LET ME OUT

A COLLECTION OF CONFESSIONS

BY

M J   J O H N S O N

Website: mjswaycreative.com

Instagram: @mjswaycreative

Tik Tok: @mjswaycreative

LET ME OUT contains sensitive content that may be distressing to some readers. Topics discussed include addiction, abuse, and suicide. The book explores these themes in a raw and emotional manner, which could evoke strong reactions and resurface painful memories for some individuals. Reader discretion is advised. If you find yourself struggling while reading this material, please prioritize your mental well-being and consider seeking support from a mental health professional or a trusted person in your life. It's okay to take breaks and prioritize self-care when reading.

I'll be here to catch you.

With love,

MJ

For all the girls –

who never thought their pain mattered

For B –

Thank you for never letting me be anyone else but myself

For my sisters –

The next generation will never know a world like this

Contents

I

Behind Closed Doors

....

"I think the saddest people always try their hardest to make people happy because they know what it's like to feel absolutely worthless and they don't want anyone else to feel like that."

—Robin Williams

welcome

And even still I tell myself, *it wasn't that bad*

This is my story

Welcome

truth

When you see my bleeding heart

My defeated soul

Splashed onto these pages

You will think to yourself

How could she do this to me

homeland

Inspired by the poet Savon Bartley
I'm from green grass and red faces
From salty air and Celtic crosses
I'm from liquor stores and Dunkin' Donuts
Greasy diners, grocery stores, and Sunday church
Sticky sap dripping off trees like honey
From caterpillars crawling on fingertips
Scraped knees, inchworms, and window exits
And *I'm going to be dead if my mom finds out*
Where everyone knows my name, my story, my family
I'm from separated fathers roaming hotel corridors
Cover my shoulders in summer like it's winter
From hot shot, packie, and *You look just like your muthah*
Several children, twenty Irish-Catholic cousins
I'm from brutal divorces after drawn-out affairs
Nannies and babysitters that raised me
From alcoholic fathers and working mothers
Fall cleanups and gardens
And white fences insulated with secrets
I'm from *Dad's out drinking again, ignore him*

....

And middle-school dances

From sunscreen and mosquito bites

From SUVs and keeping up with the Joneses

I'm from joints rolled in leaves and smoked in apples

Teenage rebellion and missed curfews

From snow days and *I'll do it if you do*

I'm the crackling fire on the first day of fall

The excitement of a snow day

And window-cleaning in spring

I'm from sleepovers, but only if I clean my room first

Country songs and high-school sweethearts

Townies and yuppies

From car crashes and motorcycle accidents

Two heart attacks and countless relapses

The game of manhunt and hide 'n' seek

Quick, kiss me! in the stairwell before Mrs. Reid sees

I'm from academics and large paychecks

I am the town that raised me

The *Why would you ever leave?*

and *When are you coming back?*

petunia

The bagged bottle of a bearded man
Martini glass of a lonely housewife
An angry boyfriend beside bottles of apologies

We think we know what it looks like
There are always signs of those like us
But no one searches for what they aren't looking for

A young addict *disappears*
One-half adult, one-half child,
Silent ghost haunting hallways
Their existence being an obvious
Foreshadow of what is yet to come

sit up straight

You can be the best sheep in the flock
The gold-star student
Button-up sweater, good posture
No original bone in your body
Seeking validation from every teacher, boss, boyfriend
Striving for someone else's acceptance
You can follow the rules your entire life
Down to the details

But at the end of the day, you're still just a follower
In a sea of sheep that look just like you
If they were walking off a cliff
You would too

daylily

My keyboard sounds like rain
I feel his presence alongside my hands
He holds my wrists so tightly his knuckles turn red
My breathing slows like a train screeching to a stop
But like a dim coal fire, my heart keeps burning
I keep typing, turning keys into thunderstorms
If I keep writing, he'll let go, he'll have to
Holding on to me is dangling from an overpass
I can make bad people go away
Just as fast as I push away the good ones
My tears well up like tiny puddles
I grit my teeth and squeak, *Leave me alone*

Then she appears like a rising sun
Leans into the curve of my neck
And whispers
Burn the whole thing down

remnants

I kneel to peer into a deserted world
In a baby-blue dress turned white
Not a white made for a bride
But a white from centuries ago
Like I'd been wearing it for decades
But I am only five
This once cinderella dress
Smells like burnt cigarettes
Blood smeared along the edges
I don't think it's my blood, or that I'm bleeding
I don't know how it happened or when
It just happened

My pink-and-purple dollhouse
Caught fire last night
I was late to a solvable crime
My dolls' faces wiped clean
Blank, empty
Remnants of make-believe personalities on the floor
I remind myself that some children never get a dollhouse

....

And big kids don't cry
So I make do with my new world
I accept things the way they are
And that I should be grateful

parentification

I toss and turn in my little bed
He falls asleep again
TV pixels flashing
I hear the Bernie and Phyl's commercial
Ear-bleeding snores I wish he'd choke on
I don't dream of eight-year-old things

Tiptoe downstairs
Hide his beers in Mom's plants
The floors are frozen
Winter in Boston hits different
When you must listen to your dad's problems
His sorrows, his trauma

We are products
Of things he won't acknowledge:
Generational trauma
Bipolar disorder
Depression
Anxiety

PTSD
Anger
Addiction
My father's pills do everything but work

He leaves the front door open again
There's a beer can on its side
He uses Mom's nice glasses
Fills them with yellow poison
That smells like urine and
Turns him into a villain
When he's supposed to be
My hero

Last week
Jessie's dad down the street
Picked her up on time
And offered me a ride
But I politely declined
I don't like the questions
These parents ask
Like, *Where is dad today?*
Or yesterday, last month, last year
I know as much as you know, buddy

I'm getting zeros on tests
I can't focus, I need rest

But he needs me
It's my responsibility
To pull blankets over bare shoulders
And click off our family's TV
Nightly routines
Just eight-year-old things
Clock turns 3:33
And I can't sleep

Am I the reason
He drinks?

strawberry blossum

I preferred hugs that felt like squishy pillows, a beautiful transaction of warmth between caretaker and child. I knew what to expect from those aging hands. I knew they would never hurt me. In my world where love was conditional, hers was not.

double digits

In the fourth grade, I decided to start swearing.
My tenth birthday was on the horizon
And it was time to act like an adult.
When I missed the soccer net at recess, it was *shit*.
When my test was covered in red ink, it was *goddamnit*.
When Treva wore the same bow as me, she was a *bitch*.

And when Dad didn't come home again, *fucking Christ*.
When Dad passed out in front of the TV, *red-faced prick*.
When Dad drove drunk with us in the car, *fucking hell*.

The teachers started whispering about me:
She's much more serious than her siblings,
Disrupts the class,
Talks too much,
Lacks focus.

In 2007 I wrote in my journal:
What a bunch of wrinkly-faced, stuck-up, stale old BITCHES.

dead man walking

There are two types of alcoholics
One is no better than the other
But if had to choose
I'd be the person who goes quick
Dies young with purpose
Rather than the one who disintegrates
In front of family and kids
With no sign of stopping
Dead man walking
Taking everyone
Down with them

3:00 AM

No one is coming

caretaking my soul

No instructions, no warning

Someone's death breathes down my neck

Pain sits in my chest like a waiting room

You're not doing enough plays on the radio

I lean on the wall, and it pulls itself back

Falling to the floor, I can't take this anymore

Stranger to my own skin, I'm doing everything I can

But I can't shake this feeling

That I'm going down with them

manic little girl

Mommy, there are termites in my brain

Crawling out of my eyes, my ears, my skin
Tiny holes in my skull, I cannot see a thing

Mommy, grab my hand
Mommy, you're sweating
Mommy, the bad people are coming
Don't let them in

When they come for me
Asking about what happened
Mommy,
Tell them
You don't know where I am

rockstar rich

A mailman fills my mailbox and nods to me.

So, kid, what do you want to be when you grow up?

I pull up a stool from the bushes and light a cigarette.

You know the guy who thought it'd be cool to build a tunnel underwater?

And the first woman to become a comedian? (Girls are much funnier than guys anyway.)

Oh, and that painter dude, the one who ripped his ear off?

He has this one quote, what was it...

I tap my fingers to my chin.

Oh, yeah: "I wish they would only take me as I am."

I wish people took me as I am. Lord knows I'd be nicer for it.

That was forever ago too, like the 1800s.

I want to be crazy enough to say timeless shit like that.

I lean back on my stool and pour Jack Daniel's into a glass cup.

With raised eyebrows and a smile, I ask, *You want some?*

Before he can answer, I keep going.

I want to be insane enough to be rich rich. Like help-others-in-times-of-need rich.

You know, the good people kind, like Oprah or Alicia Keys or P!nk.

Rockstar rich, but doing a lot of good in the world too. I want that.

I tilt my head to the sky and speak through a puff of smoke.

This place, this world we live in—it's not a fair fight.

It's not for the weak.

And I want to be the type of insane, twisted, out-of-the-box crazy enough—

I hold my cigarette to the sky and gulp down my drink.

—to believe I can change a fucking thing.

Something, anything.

Even if I can make this life a little less boring, I'll be content.

Pointing at a Lululemon family scootering by us,

I joke, *Anything but that.*

I put out my cigarette in the gravel like I'm clocking out for work,

Stand up and shake my legs as if they were asleep.

I want to be crazy for the rest of my goddamn life, I say.

I pat the mailman's shoulder—

Hope that was the answer you were looking for, dude—

And walk inside.

poker night

Once a month on Saturday nights,
The playroom transformed into a dusty Irish bar.
My desk turned into a buffet.
It's poker night, girls. Put everything away.
My friend and I anxiously awaited
This quality time with our fathers.
We played waitress and took our jobs seriously.
We erased any trace of immaturity.
This was their night, and we must not disrupt.
Men and children both at play.

My dolls put on their fishnet stockings.
My teddy bears smoked long cigarettes.
And everywhere these men went,
They silently agreed
It was their world,
This upper-middle-class world,
And we should be grateful to be in it.
We should be grateful.

The men arrived, potbellies on display.

Red faces, gold chains,

Eyes clear but never for long.

Set up the table, girls.

Don't forget the beer, girls.

Remember Richard likes his Tito's.

I was proud to serve my father and his friends.

How lucky we were that these men wanted us around.

One time I stole a plaid mini skirt from my older neighbor.

I felt like the girls in the VH1 music videos—sexy—

While the skirt clung for dear life to my birdlike bones.

If they were treating me like a woman, I wanted to look the part.

I took down orders with my flower notebook and pink pen.

You're looking so much older! Run and get me a beer.

You're going to be one heartbreaker! Honey, a glass?

*You've got yourself a little spitfire here! Fill my plate up with
whatever's out there.*

You look more like your mother each day! Sweetheart, I'll take a whiskey.

We took their orders proudly,

Swirling around like three-foot-tall fairies.

But we were ten.

We were ten.

As the night went on,

The men turned into geriatric monsters.

....

Their unfulfilled realities seeped through their bodies.

Truth spilled from their clogged pores:

Broken marriages, decades-long affairs, addictions, secrets, skeletons.

They'd talk louder and louder and louder

About their wives who openly hated them,

How they eagerly wanted sex

But never had it anymore.

Filling a glass, I thought,

When I get married, I'll always have sex with my husband.

Can't Mom just make him happy?

Can't she just do this one thing?

I shook my head and gracefully served my father his beer.

I felt sorry that their lives were so sad.

These men worked hard

For their five-bedroom houses, toys, our Catholic education.

These men were the reason I had spaghetti and meatballs,

Ice-cream cake on my birthday,

And a ten-dollar tip at the end of the night.

Hon, another one?

But we were only ten.

letters never sent I

FALL 2010

Dear B,

I sit next to Andrew Lane, and I think you're trying to make us boyfriend/girlfriend. I don't like Andrew like that. I like you, though. You're probably my favorite part of the school day. You're nice to me, and I like the way you gel your hair. Mrs. Smith doesn't really like you. Well, she doesn't really like anyone. But she picks on you a lot. You struggle to read aloud, and she still makes you. I hate when she does that. I feel your pain because I'm bad at math.

I heard you like to hang out with the older kids. And someone told me you have a girlfriend in the grade above us. I looked her up on Facebook. She's pretty. Nothing like me.

Anyway, this isn't going to go anywhere. But thanks for being nice to the new kid in school.

Maybe one day we could go to the movies.

M

supermarket flowers

You tell a child they're messy, then scold them for their knotted hair and dirty clothes

You tell a child they're disorganized, then judge them for forgetting something

You tell a child they're disgusting, then shame them for their indulgences

You tell a child they're stupid, then gasp at their lack of devotion to anything

If you teach a child they're not worthy enough times, they'll believe it

They'll believe they were born broken, different

And in order to survive, they'll seek out anything to escape

The reality you gave them

Straight up

suburban secrets

Each mansion on Wood Street
Has its own story

Dan four houses down
Used to down
Two bottles of whiskey
In an evening
He married his nanny
Till she had to leave
Making his family of four
A family of three

Now the Lees
Are a different story
Pen was a nurse
Mike worked on State Street
Appeared to be happy
But Mike liked the ladies
So their family of four
Became a family of three

Then Pen remarried
And this man
This man was a treat
He kept her on a leash
And their family of three
Became a family of seven
And now Pen
Must be home by eleven
Or else, he threatens
And she asks herself
What happened
To the life she imagined
In this mansion

Kacey lives alone
Soft-spoken woman
Dressed in brown
She moved here
When I was two
And people talk in town
Say she isn't allowed
To leave her house
And people found out
That Kacey
Is really named Stacey

And she created this secret reality
To hide her sexuality

The most attractive on the block
Are Ellie and Paul Lock
She dresses in diamonds
Gave him three kids
And even though Ellie
Has legs like heaven
And stands at five-foot-eleven
A straight man's haven
It doesn't make a difference
Because Paul likes the attention
Of men, not women
Now every night she dreams
Of a ring that means something

A house at the dead end
Lived the Wilsons
One wife, one husband
Three kids were rambunctious
Dad, an addict
And the mom appeared
Absent, distracted
Turned out, she was saving
So she could leave him

And take her children

Far away

From this street

And teach them

What it means

To be free

deadbeat

Duffel bag thrown over your shoulder

Kissed us on our foreheads

Said, *Take care of your mother*

listen up girls

"Why can't you do anything right?"

"Do you ever think about anyone else but yourself?"

"What did you expect when this is how you dress?"

"You couldn't just do this one thing?"

"She's so easy."

"Don't you think you've had enough?"

"What did you do to provoke him?"

"I raised you better than this."

"You're going to waste a pretty face."

"No one will want to be with you if you act like that."

"Just do it for me."

"How are you going to take care of kids one day?"

"How are you going to take care of a husband one day?"

"All that food is going to catch up to you."

"Some kids have nothing. Be grateful."

"That is what you're wearing?"

"Show some respect."

"After everything I've done for you?"

"You're going to eat all of that?"

"Would it kill you to smile?"

"What do you have to be sad for?"

....

cold case

I assembled a search party
Drew maps of all the places you could be
Put fliers on every post, bulletin board, and storefront
Missing—if found, please return to my family

I told the news to tell the news
Looked behind every door
Peeked under mattresses
Tore apart closets
Screamed your name in the streets
Till my knees hit pavement and
My voice became weak
Where did you go?
Please come home

At age twelve, I couldn't comprehend
That you weren't missing
You left

conditional jesus

Once when I skipped Sunday mass, an old wrinkly woman said to me, *God gives you seven days. You can give him one.*

She also told me never date a man who isn't white, that if I have sex before marriage no man will ever propose to me, and if don't cover my shoulders I will end up like the girl across the street.

I didn't know what that meant. I didn't know any people of color. I didn't even know the girl across the street. All I knew was I hated going to that church, I hated the people in that church, and I hated the way this woman talked about other people.

So all I could think in my thirteen-year-old brain was, *shut the fuck up lady*.

LoLz

letters never sent II

WINTER 2011

Dear B,

It's February vacation and I'm stuck in my room. It's been four days since break started and you still haven't messaged me. I thought we'd gotten closer these last few months. I consider you one of my best friends. And when you and your girlfriend broke up, I thought you'd want to spend more time with me. You even promised we'd go to the movies this week.

Anyway, just writing this to tell you that I won't talk to you ever again. When we get back to science class, I'll sit somewhere else.

Don't text me.

M

skeleton

I find solace in these four periwinkle walls
And deep-plum carpets
I think my pale-pink legs will turn deep purple
Every time I touch my toes to its soft surface
The minuscule lock on this golden doorknob
Is my best friend, my accomplice, in the fight for my life
The fight to survive a life no one needs saving from
Or that's what they think, that's what we know

I click the lock and dive into my own reality
Books, hidden journals, explicit websites
Alcohol, promiscuous text messages
This is the world inside my world
From the inside looking out, I send signals: *H E L P*
As if Batman himself would find his way to my doorstep

When I open that door, I can hear the fighting
This home is an NYC subway station
The train is delayed by eighteen years
No one knows anyone, anymore
People walk by without a mere hello
A castle rotten through its teeth

. . . .

Children's laughter, innocent pranks replaced with
Deafening silence or irrefutable warfare
My mother's china shattered on frozen floors
Wilted flowers in a colorful garden turned gray
This house is a skeleton of what it used to be

A Christmas tree lies horizontal on a decaying rug
No more VH1 Top 20 Countdowns, pancakes, and dancing
A man who was once my hero, now a confusing patient
He is the nucleus of this vacant mansion

I walk barefoot down empty hallways
Bang on the walls, shout their names
But no one cares to listen to a child
Who is told she doesn't know anything

And when the palace starts to shake
I slip into my room, hear the lock click
Kneel beside my bed and pray
I'll make it out of here one day

woody

Woody was a bad boy. He wore a gold chain, dressed in skinny jeans, and leaned his chair back during class. He had one earring that I loved to twirl around with my fingertips. He smelled like Axe body spray, wore faded t-shirts, and made my insides light up like fireworks. The kids would tease Woody, saying his mom was a MILF. I didn't know what that was, but it made him red-faced and violent, ready to knock those kids out.

His stepdad Dave had just moved in. Dave liked to drink. One day Woody admitted that Dave would get drunk and hit his mom. When this happened, Woody hid his little siblings in the closet. He protected them. I liked that about him. If I was ever in trouble, I would call Woody.

Woody and I would sit in the back of the bus. One rainy afternoon on the ride home, Woody and I sunk low so the driver couldn't see us. Woody promised that he'd take the blame if we got caught. So we put our foreheads together, then our mouths. It wasn't my first kiss, but it was electric. His lips were like watermelon candy. I dreamed of running away with Woody, getting the next train to Boston and taking his little siblings with us.

....

We talked about my dreams more than his. Woody wanted me to succeed so badly but accepted he would never leave. One night, I got drunk before the school dance. I hated the taste and swore I'd never do it again, but my belly felt warm and my head felt like a pop concert. In a way, I felt like Woody—rebellious, free from any consequences.

When Woody realized I wasn't myself, he pulled me to the corner of the dance floor like you would a screaming toddler. With eyes so big I thought they'd fall out of his beautiful face, he said, *You're going places, M. You're smart. You can't start this stuff. Don't drop the ball, M. You've got to get out of here.* In that moment, I realized Woody wasn't himself either.

A few weeks later, Woody started missing school for days at a time. And eventually, he stopped coming altogether. For months I put my backpack on the open seat beside me on the bus, just in case he showed up. I told myself, *Woody will come to my house, tell me he missed me, let me ride on his bike pegs, and then take me to get ice cream.* In the same breath, I worried about Dave. I hated Dave. I hated that he might've taken Woody away from me.

For the next few years, Woody was in and out of foster care. He struggled with his own addictions. He spent time in and out of youth detention centers. I wish someone would've protected Woody as much as he protected me.

And he was right. I had the ball—until I dropped it.

....

letters never sent III

SPRING 2011

Dear B,

I can't believe it's the end of middle school. Remember when you ditched me over February break, and I didn't talk to you for a week? By that Friday, you were so frustrated. Right there in front of everyone, you grabbed my hips and made me face you. That was the first time you touched me, and I think my heart exploded into butterflies.

We've spent the last two years attached to the hip. When Mrs. Reid caught us kissing in the stairwell, you took the fall and said, 'We weren't doing anything; we were just saying goodbye.' She believed it and didn't call our parents. But when we did get caught, we somehow managed to get detention while already in detention. The teacher caught us passing notes underneath our desks, and we both swallowed back laughter as she read them aloud to us.

We spent hours on the phone after school, chatting about our days and giggling on our pillows. I smoked weed for the first time with my best friend Taylor, and you were so mad that I didn't wait for you. We sat on gigantic rocks by the water and talked for hours. You would tell me you were going to marry me someday. That we were only fourteen, but you had no interest in meeting another girl. You'd jokingly sing 'You are the best thing that has ever been mine' and kiss me on the cheek. I'd roll my eyes, but you knew I loved hearing that. We slept over our friends' houses so we could sneak out of windows and make out in the woods. We danced at school dances, and Mr. Lynn kicked us out for hugging too much. He made us sit in the hallway and shamelessly wait for our parents to pick us up. We were so rebellious and carefree that I didn't have to think about what was going on behind closed doors.

When my dad got sick, I spent nearly three months at the hospital after school. You kept noticing how tired I was. My phone calls came in later, but you stayed up. Some nights we'd be awake until three am, and your mom would come in periodically to yell at you for being up. I wasn't allowed to tell anyone why he was in there; I didn't really know why he was, but it was bad. He couldn't read or write anymore; he barely knew my name. I knew he almost died but didn't know why. You let me cry on the phone night after night and begged me to confess what was going on. One night, I squeaked out, 'My dad is really sick, and no one is supposed to know.' You didn't press any longer; you just sat there, quietly. Your presence in silence was all I needed. I wanted to tell you everything. But I couldn't. It wasn't anyone else's business.

I survived middle school because of you. B. I walked in knowing no one and I'm leaving with a pool of people that I love so much. I hate that I'm going back to Catholic school, 45 minutes away. I just got comfortable, and now I'm leaving.

Today, we are going to the beach with our friends. I put together this scrapbook of us. I hope you like it.

I love you, B. You are the best thing that has ever been mine.

HAGS,

M

survival protocol

Footsteps sting my ears

Heart races

I wipe my swollen eyes with sheets

Stifle breathing

A statue in place of a child

She's asleep, they yell back

fools

Pointing fingers at artists
With ankles chained to their seats

disposable

I'm the food stuck between your teeth
An old takeout tray and empty soda cans
I'm the rusty razor head glued to the tub
A toothbrush with frayed bristles
The gum at the bottom of your shoe
I'm the expired milk in the back of the fridge
The *I'll get to it later* and the *do it yourself*
I'm the eye roll, the *ugh*, the *what now?*
The reason you must leave early
I'm your punching bag
Your inconvenience
A mirror to your failed achievements
I am what you treat me like I am
Disposable

voicemail

Hey Dad,

I heard you and Mom's wedding song

In the grocery store today,

"Faithfully" by Journey.

How've you been?

How's Florida?

I guess it's been a year now.

I didn't make varsity, just JV.

Feels pointless to try when you're not here

To give me notes on what I did well

And what I didn't.

Your friends keep asking where you went,

Said you haven't been answering their calls.

I think they miss you.

I think I miss you too.

Are you ever coming back?

You tell me you're happier there,

You're sober now,

You help your new girlfriend around the house.

....

I thought we would've been enough to stay.

Anyway, sorry for this long message.

I just wish you were here.

We could hit the gym

Or see the new Will Ferrell movie.

Well, I'll catch you another time.

Love you. Bye.

thomas

You weren't there

When I slipped into the hands of another villain

Your opponent: a high school boyfriend

This time my age, twice my size

A troubled boy who believed men were better than women

Who sucked out any self-love I had left after you left

Placed it in a locked box

With a key that never existed

He told me careless nothings in my ear

Words that wrapped around my body like a python

Making sure I was controlled

Hey, this is a little tight

Making sure I couldn't decide

I don't think we should do this

Making sure I was his

I'll do anything you say

boomerang

I thought my life was ruined when you left

I was wrong

My life was ruined the day you came back

academia

She slides the 54 facedown on the desk
You keep this up, you're not going far
Should I tell her what's going on?
That I slept in my car last night
Because I didn't want to go home
Or missed class last week
Because he struggled to breathe
And the EMTs were asking me
Questions I can't repeat
Maybe I should tell her
I'm so fucking tired
From washing his sheets
Making sure he eats
Charging his ankle bracelet while he sleeps
So the cops don't show up
So he doesn't go away again
Homework doesn't fit with codependence
Maybe I should confess: I'm terrified
That I'll walk in on his death

And I can't do a damn thing about it
Perhaps she'll understand, lend a hand
To a teenager who's not going to go far
But instead, I dig my nails into my thighs
Swallow tears down like medicine
Ask, *What's the extra credit?*

I was told

To cover up
Only to be ripped wide open

people pleaser

I don't know which question is scarier:
Do you like this?
Or
Are you okay with this?
When I've only been taught to answer
Yes.

covered in everything

Like stitches sewn into skin
Their words are scars on my soul
Messy written on my neck
Bad branded on my forehead
Ungrateful lining my collarbone
Hopeless engraved on my lower belly
Whore carved into my thighs
Crazy burned along my fingertips
Secondary inscribed on my palms

Their words sting
Like venomous bites
From a species that lives
Where no one thinks to look

Their words make me feel
Like I'm topless
In front of a hungry crowd
Covered in everything
They taught me I was

⟨♡⟩ all-american girl

Alice was crafted by the American gods. She came from old New England money, the kind of money trail that should be in museums. Generational wealth with a reputation you'd kill yourself over.

She had long blonde hair, blue eyes, porcelain skin that turn golden in the summertime, and an athletic build. Tall but not too tall, not too muscular but you could tell she played sports: soccer in the fall, track in the winter, and lacrosse in the spring. Varsity on all three.

Someone was always patting Alice on the back. High school boys admired her innocence, validated her as "wifey material." P*lease* and *thank you* were her love languages. She never needed makeup because her beauty came naturally. Her clothes covered anything that might lead to a man's arousal. She went to church on Sundays, taught CCD, and volunteered for kids in her free time. Alice loved kids. People would tell her, *You're going to be such a good mom one day*.

She never raised her voice, never talked back, or gave anyone a hard time. She prided herself on being agreeable and always smiling. Alice never wanted to make anyone uncomfortable because that would be rude, and good girls aren't rude. Even when she felt her cheeks flush and that dirty feeling rise in her belly, she'd give an anxious laugh and say something appropriate and digestible: *Okay. Yeah. Sure. I'm sorry.* The only responses she was allowed.

Alice aspired to be a nurse, a schoolteacher, or a social worker. When people asked about her future, she'd respond politely, *I just want to help people.* Alice loved Jesus. She swore to her friends that she would never drink, do drugs, steal, or have sex before marriage. Alice judged any kid that sipped from the glass of teenage rebellion. She thought it was ungrateful that a child would go against the hand that feeds them. Alice was always *grateful*.

And Alice was incredibly smart. She'd known she wanted to be a Princeton Tiger since she was seven. Her father and mother met at Princeton Law. Well, her mom was in law school until she got pregnant, dropped out, and became a full-time mom. Her dad went on to graduate, land a six-figure salary in the 90s, and become a partner by age thirty. Alice was on that track: AP calculus, AP government, AP chemistry. Her dad's approval was everything to her. After all, he works hard to provide for his family, and she was going to make him proud.

Alice's life was decided years before she even took her first breath. On paper, you'd think Alice was born into choice, but she only had one. One way to act, one way to behave, one way to love. One.

We all have a little Alice in us.

horror

I always wondered why my father threw tantrums
About attending Sunday mass
I worried he would go to hell if he didn't
(As if he wasn't already there)
Now I know why he didn't want to go
And I don't blame him

3:13 AM

I wake up to my own scream, with droplets of sweat covering my forehead. I trace the cross dangling from my neck as I watch the monsters celebrate on my walls.

Close my eyes and pray, *Please, do not let him die.*

letters never sent IV

SPRING 2015

Dear B,

I was out by the water last night, sitting on the same rocks, drinking a beer, and letting my mind drift to memories. I've lived a hundred lives since we were fourteen, and I hate that I never let you be a part of them. You are the only love I know.

I lasted three months into freshman year before I realized who I was would not survive in this school. It wasn't cool to date or even talk to public school kids; you had to have designer everything, and it was embarrassing to be from a town like ours, not known for money. So I sat back, watched, and learned the ropes before I covered up everything about my upbringing. These girls were so rich, B. The entire parking lot filled with BMWs, Mercedes, and brand-new jeeps. I drive a 2004 Explorer; old Red is heard rolling down the parking lot every morning. You'd love it. You will love it.

The last time we saw each other was on New Year's during freshman year. We broke up when I started the new school, thinking it was for the best. But, of course, the text messages started soon after we stopped talking. That night, our friend's parents weren't home, so we drank and danced until the new year. When everyone was asleep, we snuck into a bedroom and made out for hours. We weren't ready to have sex yet, but we talked about it. We knew we wanted to be each other's first. You reassured me that wherever I go, I'll always be the person you want to marry. I wrote you a letter the day after, sealed it with some lipstick, and handed it to Taylor to put in your locker. When you called me before school started again, you said, 'You already wrote me a letter, didn't you?'

Then, I disappeared. I got wrapped up in being popular in this new school. I stopped responding to your messages and became a stranger in your life. I tossed our delicate love to the side and chased superficial acceptance by rich kids. But eventually, I found friends who were like us and we survived the school together. I lost my virginity to this boy that I didn't care about and broke up with him weeks after. Only to fall into the hands of a controlling boyfriend who made me feel so small I lost my voice. Can you imagine that? Me, losing my voice? If you, or any of our old friends knew him, you boys would've made sure he left me alone. However, I won't tell you this. It's my own business, and I took care of it anyways.

....

My dad ended up leaving for two years but eventually he came back. I've spent the last year of high school being his caretaker, watching him disintegrate in front of my eyes. Racing home after school to make sure he took his meds, changing his sheets, and grocery shopping. I fear that he won't be able to survive when I leave for college. He is about to lose his business too, and then I don't know what is left. I won't tell you this either, I can't. I'm taking care of it anyways.

I tracked your life all throughout high school; thank God we have Instagram and Facebook. It looks like you're happy. It looks like I shouldn't rock the boat. But I can't help it, I want to hear your voice. I want to apologize for the time that is lost.

I took another swig of my beer and let it hit my belly before sending the text.

When I asked if you knew who this was, you responded, "Of course I do."

M

insidious attention

It's like fists on my back
Pushing against my mattress
It's been months with this insidious attention
Like an open wound you ignore till it's infected
And maggots start to crawl from your skin

I scream into my pillow, *Go away*
Like a child who doesn't want to go to school
Not tonight, I promise I'll be good
I'll do what I should
Not that I know what it wants

My mattress lies still for a moment
A moment between relief and terror
I peek over my sheets to the periwinkle floor
A women's bruised hand appears from underneath
Slides gently across the carpet
Her skin is translucent, as if one pinch would reveal bone
Monsters aren't real, I whisper to myself
I slip down the side of the bed with caution

. . . .

She fits her bones into my warm hand
Her touch is ice cold yet motherly, gentle

For a moment, I do not fear her
I meet her tear-filled blue eyes
She is a confusing mixture of my father and mother
Dirt covers her arms like crumbs of chocolate cake
Like she's come crawling out of a grave
Her soaked white dress smells like swamp
Leeches cover her neck
She reveals a bloody smile
I gasp at the sight, she does the same
Curly blonde hair drapes over her shoulders, dripping

With my free hand, I twist the blonde curls on my head
And watch as she grabs hers too
Who are you?
Her muddy lip quivers as she begins to sob

Her grip grows stronger
She pulls our faces closer
My pale hands turn red, swelling every second
My heart begins to pound in my ears
She puts her chin on my shoulder and whispers
Run

....

little one

You cannot wait
For them to set you free

boston boy

Throw me over his shoulder
Meg, come on, get in the water
Pull a joint from my pocket
Oh, you think you're a stonah, kehd?

I give him a light push, a giggle
He pokes and teases, *huh kehd?*

Backwards hat baby
One hand on the old chevy
Worn-in carpet bucket seats
You're too far away, ride next to me

Right hand around my waist
You know I'm going to marry you one day?

Hungover mornings, off to Dunkin'
Put your wallet away, you're not paying
Knows his way around any engine
My boston boy can fix anything

....

I laugh, *the music is so loud, what?*
He smiles, *this song reminds me of us!*

He waits for me to curl up on his lap
Smells like salt water, beer, and sweat
The calloused hands of a working man
I can't wait to buy my own land

I'm infatuated with his reckless nature
Did you tell your mom you're staying ovah?

He leans his head back, *I love the trees*
Catches my *I love you so much* gaze
I want to say,
You know I'm going to marry you one day?

september

I'll pour this summer
Into a glass bottle
Take it with me
Take you with me
Wherever I go
I'll open it come September
Just to hear your laugh
I promise
I'll see you again
I promise

stay a little longer

When I saw your truck rolling down my street, I put on the cutest sundress and ran out the door. As you pulled into the driveway, I texted my mother, *be home late, don't wait up*. You were wearing a backwards hat and had a childish grin on your face. I hopped in the front seat and gave you a big kiss on the cheek. Although we hadn't seen each other in years, I knew this was going to be the best summer of my life.

You looked the same as me: *relieved*. Whenever we were together, we felt like kids again. We found instant joy within our polarities. I thought we were off to the water, but we were going to the fields instead. I trusted you behind the wheel. I knew wherever we went, you'd keep me safe. There was a six-pack in the backseat, a rolled joint in the cup holder, and a blanket that could only mean one thing. We hadn't seen each other in years, yet here we were. Two people no one would've put together. A connection that we couldn't explain. Were us, B.

I fell madly in love with you that summer. When you took me mudding, I laughed so hard that my cheeks went numb, and my ribs hurt. You tossed your head back in laughter as you watched me grip the door handle for dear life. "Oh, it's not scary! I could do this in my sleep!" you said as we were driving vertically up a dirt-covered bump. Everything in your world was an adventure. You said I needed to jump in the swimming hole before I left for college, like it was a rite of passage. I was terrified of the musty, swamp-like water. But with enough of your encouragement, I jumped. I remember the split-second underwater silence, thinking, "I love this boy so much."

We made love in your truck outside of our friend's place. You showed up to my graduation party, a little shy and awkward because it was the first time I let you come over. It didn't take you too long to get comfortable. You spent an hour in my living room, combing through childhood photos of me, laughing and pointing, saying, "that's my wild child." It was as if you had just discovered a treasure chest filled with all the hidden parts of me. I loved that you came, but I didn't love that you were in my house. You were too precious to be in this place; I feared you'd notice the cracks in the walls.

We jumped off bridges into ice-cold water. After spending days beneath the sun, we'd just drive, feeling sleepy and high. With country music playing softly in the background and your hand on my thigh, I didn't want to be anything but yours. Nothing else mattered in those moments.

....

We could barely keep up with falling in love, never mind the thought of being apart. We danced underneath the trees at night. The boat was a portal to deep conversations about where we were going and where we didn't want to go. We never talked about my life at home, but we both understood it was bad. For me, college was the only option. I was headed to South Carolina in the fall.

We talked about you leaving, I think we both knew it would never happen. You were chained to this place while I was merely tied to it. We spent those last few weeks entangled in each other. We didn't realize we'd always be running out of time or making up for time.

A piece of my heart is locked in that summer we were eighteen. I think loving you was the last innocent thing I ever did.

II

Pretending is a Grueling Sport

....

"I'm standing in the ashes of who I used to be."

— Halsey, "Angel on Fire"

king street

There's blood in this city
And we're all swimming in it
Drowning under the illusion
Of what it means to be young

metal chains

Throughout each season
I'll numb myself with anything

letters never sent V

FALL 2015

Dear B,

The memory of our last night together is still fresh, like an open wound that refuses to heal properly. It hurts to touch. On my last day home, I wanted to spend every waking moment with you. We spent the day on the water, not saying a whole lot. The doom of goodbye lurked over our heads, and we had long pockets of silence. We weren't equipped to handle this type of goodbye.

I had waited my whole life to move out of this town, and here I was, wishing I could call the move off. I prayed someone would give me a permission slip to stay. My heart wanted to be with the boy I was in love with, live in the town that raised me, and hold on to the friends that took care of me. But it didn't matter what I wanted; I didn't have any other options but to leave. Although I lived in a house with five bedrooms, there is no room. I had to go. We hugged, kissed, and cried in my driveway until 3 AM, holding on to each other with all our strength, deep down knowing that too many things are about to change.

I made you a scrapbook of all our memories and put them in a mason jar, with a letter telling you I loved you. It was the first time I said it, and I didn't let myself see you open it. What if you didn't feel the same way? But you did, you always have.

It's been a few weeks since we last spoke. We tried to talk every day once I got down here. I'd talk about my classes, the friends I was making, the parties. You would keep me updated on what was going on back home. After a few weeks went by, the calls started getting further apart. I was studying the character I needed to create to survive in this new environment. I left you behind in the noise of it all. Apparently, having a boy back in your hometown wasn't something you did. I knew waiting for me to come home was never an option. Even if it was, we never talked about it. Then again, I never asked you to visit. I just left, open ended.

After a few months, I heard through the grapevine that you were seeing someone. I had no right to be so upset, but I couldn't stomach the thought of us being officially over, even though I had you at arm's length. When you said you two were hanging out, I smashed the photo of us, the one on your truck bed, me in my red Converse. It's one of my favorite memories. We planned on doing something that afternoon but just sat there for hours talking about life, losing track of time in each other was our specialty.

B, we talked about this. How you were going to get out and move on like me. California, North Carolina... anywhere but there. But you didn't. You never give yourself a second to be alone. You never give yourself a chance to figure out what you want.

I don't remember what I said on the phone. I didn't let you hear me cry. I didn't want you to think I cared that much. I didn't tell you that missing you felt like missing limbs. I should've told you how I loathed school with every ounce of my being. That I was completely lost in this new city with these new friends. That I hated it here too, or hated who I was becoming here. All of it's too much for me: the drinking, the drugs, the work. I'm so broke, and these classes are easy to miss. It's loud here, B. I wish I could've gone to school closer to home, closer to you. I know I said I hate it there, but hating something you can't have is easier than longing for it. It's incredibly lonely when you can't go home anymore. My family wants me far away, now that I have a chance to start over. If I told them what I really wanted, who I wanted, I don't think they'd ever support it. But I didn't tell you this.

I put on this façade in hopes that you'd leave too. I jumped in first so you would know the water was warm, like you did for me at the swimming hole. I didn't want you to know I was miserable. I didn't want you to know how unhappy I was without you. I didn't know how to tell you that, so I stopped responding to everything. I shut you out of my life and put you in my box of "never talk to agains."

....

79

Until I got your letter in the mail this week. Thank you. I needed to know you were feeling the same way. I don't know why I can't tell you how I feel without you telling me first. Thank you for the bracelets too. I'm wearing them to class now. It's like you're here with me.

I'm trying to convince my mom to buy my plane ticket home this weekend so I can come see you. We have a lot to talk about. I'm not letting you off the hook that easy. I miss you like crazy, B.

See you soon,

M

beach weekend

He sniffs fairy dust off my breasts
I react with a devilish grin
Let's do it in the bathroom
His eyebrows raise as if his girlfriend
Is the kinkiest thing about him
And I am

In my tiny lingerie, I take his hand
Desire is my hungriest obsession
Sexuality is the only expression I comprehend
I'm having fun with his attention
Art in live action

When he touches his effect on me
It covers his fingers
I whisper, *See what you do to me?*
He lifts my hips onto the dirty sink
His tongue dances around my body
Forcing my head back

As he flips me over, the party echoes
I catch a glimpse of myself in the mirror
Heavy eyeliner
Long blonde hair bouncing with every thrust
A rockstar's girlfriend

I'm bad and he treats me like it
His sex is electric static
He digs his name in my back
A silent warning to others that
He was here

clones

What a tragedy it is
To be around people
Who are all the same

word

criminal

I reach for things
I can't put down,
The push and pull
Of the unavailable.
Glass-covered floors,
Jealous fists through a door—
This addictive personality
Will get you before it gets me.
Yellow electricity
Will steal your stability.
Make me the air you breathe.

Now you reach for things
You can't put down.

broken bird

Your father couldn't stay

Your mother never wanted you anyway

I'm the only one who will ever love you

Your wrinkles, those freckles, that awful tattoo

To most people, you're not worth it

But me? I find you perfect

Come here, come close, I'll keep you warm

Together we can get through any storm

But never forget all the things you lack

Because I'm the only one who will love you back

hypocrite

I'm sitting in my therapist's office
Wine stains on my lips from the night before
Crying about an alcoholic father who doesn't love me

I don't know what's scarier
The fact that she didn't realize
Or just how good I was at hiding it

3:15 AM

There is not enough water in the ocean to wash the guilt off me.

bloodshot eyes

When I look at you,

All I see is him:

Bloodshot eyes,

Gold chain.

My mind can't tell the difference.

And it's not you, it's me.

He's still haunting me in my sleep.

lilith

You love me the way a child loves candy:

With a short-lived obsession.

You try to make me healthy and sustainable,

Squeezing every ounce of creativity and impulse out of me.

Like clay stuck between your fingertips,

I'll conform for a little while.

For a little while, I'll be whatever you need me to be.

I'll let you believe,

That someone with the personality of a ruptured artery,

Could survive a life of predictability.

You'll have me till you don't,

Till I save enough money and take the first flight out.

I'll warn you every step of the way,

But you won't listen. You won't believe me when I say,

I'm not a high school trophy collecting dust.

I'm not a homecooked meal. I'm not a caretaker.

I'm not somebody's mother.

I don't feel like we're meant for forever.

I'm a lesson to make you realize

....

What love is and isn't.

I'll stay loyal until I hate you,

Until I cheat on you,

Until I gut you,

Never to be the same again,

All because you decided to love someone

Who doesn't love you back.

letters never sent VI

WINTER 2017

Dear B,

Last night was the first time I'd seen you in two years. You look the same but different. Your boyish features are dwindling, yet you're still eighteen.

After visiting you in the fall of freshman year, I knew we were done. So, when I got your call about breaking it off, I wasn't shocked. You chose someone more convenient, and I didn't choose you at all. I didn't let myself. I didn't try to bring you into my new world. I didn't try, B.

By the time I came home, school was getting better. I was making friends and adjusting to the party scene. I guess I've adjusted well my whole life. I morph myself into whatever helps me fit in. Seems like every time I turn a corner, I change my colors again. But with you, I don't have to be anyone else. I get a break from the character I'm playing, and I'm me again.

I have a boyfriend now, a fraternity boy from a rich family. I'm dating him because he fits into the person I'm being. He's the type of boy who wouldn't know how to change a tire, and I hate that so much. I know you still have a girlfriend. After two long years, I've accepted that we were just another summer romance. But we both know; pretending is a grueling sport. Numbing the hole in our hearts is easier than admitting it's there.

I knew you'd be at this party. I planned to keep my distance, but I could feel your eyes on the back of my neck the entire time. You were on the counter, not trying to talk to the people you didn't care about. Everyone thinks you're so shy. I've always found that amusing, how people could miss all your dimensions, layers, dramas. Getting to know the real you is like gaining entry to an exclusive club. You're the opposite of me in that way.

After a couple of drinks, we sat down next to each other and picked up right where we'd left off. Under tacky Christmas lights, amid drunk childhood friends, and back in this cold town, we were somehow in that summer again.

When it was time to go, you begged me for just another hour. It was getting late, and I only had one ride home. After teasing back and forth you grabbed my wrist and asked shyly, "What if you stayed the night?" I raised my eyebrows in shock, tilted my head and said, "Nothing good will come out of me staying over." Admittedly, there was nowhere else I'd rather be than in this living room that smelled like menthols and stale beer. When I gave you the tightest hug goodbye, memory drifted to that last night in my driveway, and tears began to well up in my eyes. You smelled like pine trees, like a fire you could start out of nothing.

As the car pulled out of the driveway, your name shined brightly on my phone.

I don't know when I'll get another moment with you, B. It is pure torture not knowing when you'll see someone you love again.

M

cape cod

It was snowing in the bathroom
So we tiptoed to the bedroom
Put your head on my stomach
My fingers dancing in your hair
Like a million times before
I didn't tell you I was leaving
This time, this town
Knowing damn well
Love doesn't grow in a triangle

wake the fuck up dad

I hear echoes of his snores
My arms pace back and forth
Sweat drips from my forehead
As I scrub his insides off
This old toilet seat

He moved closer to me
When I was 20
There aren't enough highways to separate
A father who relies on his daughter
To attend his every waking need

My hands move faster as rage
Fills my belly, I try not to get sick
But I already am, I already have been
Generational addiction

The bristles on the sponge flare
Tears drip down my cheeks

....

I hate everything about this man
Taste salt on my lips – *I'm still just a kid*

My whole life I've been
pressed against a wall of a crowded room
with people who are more important than me
And even if I wanted to
I wouldn't tell them the truth
That my mind is broken too

I flush the bubbles and watch
As they swirl into the unknown
I dream of going down with them
Lean back, face the now clean surface
And start to bawl quiet, fearful sobs

morning after

Snow came

In September

Thank god

You don't remember

Cause my phone

Missed the wall

Hit your face

And my anger

Destroyed our place

june in new england

I worked a double that day. Exhaustion set in at night.

Grabbed the neck of a bottle like a desperate husband,

Didn't bother to take off my apron.

Sat on the floor of my closet, sobbing.

Speaking to the leather belt on a hanger:

In a few moments, this can all be over.

logan

Holding a musician's hand

Is like quicksand

Into the land of the living

kerosene

The hair on the back of my neck stands up
I cover my mouth as if that will stop
The words I'm about to spit out
You're not as fast as I am
Not as quick with your words
Terrible at reassurance
You won't tell me you're not cheating
So I wait for one wrong response
One melancholic remark
An *I don't care what happen*s attitude
Or worse, silence
And then I'll lose it
Flip this table over
Slam doors, break dishes
Pull out your insecurities and shortfalls
Play tug-of-war with your insides
Become a giant who lights this house on fire
At any sign of a spark or crack
And I'll happily walk away
While it burns

senses

You're touching my body
Smelling my neck
Tasting my tongue
And hearing my voice
I don't feel you
And I don't care to

hourglass

An addict is a perfectionist
In a straitjacket
Sitting in front of an hourglass
Filled with unfinished art

unsatisfied

My eyes dry out as daylight pulses through the windows

How dare the sun shines when all I want is rain

Yet when the rain rushes in, ready to pour

I curse the sun for leaving

letters never sent VII

Dear B,

Two days after that Christmas party, I called you up, crying. Although you were at some crowded townie bar, you answered on the first ring. By the tone of your voice, I knew you were feeling it too. Seeing each other again reassured us of what we had known all along: we still love each other. We are still in love with each other. It's been months of back and forth since that phone call, a purgatory of decisions we are terrified of making.

I've tried to move on in every possible way. But everyone I've met feels disposable, detachable, like a quick fix to make me forget who's back home. I know in my bones that you do not love her. I know if I stayed, it would be me waking up next to you. It would be me. I know family politics influence every decision in our lives, but eventually, we are going to have to make a decision for us. Sometimes this love story makes me hate you. It makes me hate her. And it makes me hate myself.

I'll tell you that, and you expect it. Love can't survive in a triangle: one person is stuck, one person is in the dark, and the other one is alone.

Fortunately for you, my hatred is fleeting, and soon I'm loving you again. I'll send a message into a black hole, never knowing if you're alone, if you'll respond, or when we'll connect again.

I felt a buzz in my pocket just as I arrived at a pregame. We messaged back and forth throughout the night, and when I got back to my room, you called me. With each sentence, I morphed back into myself. Your voice is home. I wish I could listen to it in the weeks when I don't hear from you at all. I wish I could listen to it now.

Last night, your tone shifted, and with determination and confidence, you asked me to come home. "Meg, come home so we can get married," a line with which I am all too familiar by now, yet never get tired of hearing. Your voice had a slight hint of annoyance in it, as if my reluctance to move back home was equivalent to a child who doesn't want to leave the playground. You knew before I did that home was what I needed more than ever. I think we had an unspoken agreement that I was drifting too far, and it was starting to get dangerous.

"I know I tease, but I've always been serious about this. Come home so we can finally get married," as casually as asking me to close a window.

We dreamed up our life in the middle of the night. I told you I can't move back home, so we chose somewhere neutral: North Carolina. Two kids, dogs, chickens, dirt bikes. A small house (you remembered I hate big houses) and a huge backyard with a swing. A screened-in porch so I could write outside throughout all seasons, and a dusty fireplace. *Our floors would creak with every memory made.* We'd grow our own vegetables and have a colorful garden with blue hydrangeas, carnations, and roses. I'd always keep an orchid on the windowsill. We'd spend our nights belly laughing and chasing curly-headed barefoot children around.

While we were talking, I swear I could smell the fresh cut grass and the ocean breeze roaming through our dream house. *This future was a sunny walk down a familiar street, and we treated it like an impossible illusion.*

When the morning sun peered through our windows, the dread of saying goodbye washed over me. You bluffed that you'd get in your truck and drive fifteen hours to come get me. I giggled and sheepishly said, "No, you can't, I'll be home soon enough." I should've pushed you further. I should've met you somewhere. I should've let you take me away from this new life and put me back in my old one. But I didn't. I held your hand with space between our fingertips. I knew you were looking for reassurance that if you blew your life up, I would stand by you. But I can never bring myself to promise you that. "A flight risk," you called me.

Today, you're a ghost to me again. All I'm left with is an old playlist and a daydream of our drawn-out future.

Till next time, B. Whenever that will be.

M

seduction

We love to raise eyebrows
At things we shouldn't do
Surge of *yes*
Rushing through us
Dancing on ledges over
Shark-infested waters
Seduced by a cigarette
Powerless to sweat
Dripping down
A wine glass
Planning on B because
A is too boring
Too predictable
Makes our eyes glaze
So we gaze, tongue-kissing
Self-destructing
Breaking
Everything

benders

I wake up hazy
Swollen eyes
A headache that's a motherfucker
I scan the room
Trying not to wake the stranger
Sleeping peacefully in my bed
Chris? Brandon? Evan?
Shake the names out of my head
When he wakes up
I'll ask to put his number in my phone
Works every time

17 missed calls, 10 texts, 2 percent battery
My phone has more life in it than I do
I remember some things but regret everything
Where are you? from Shane
Answer your phone from Brian
You're literally the worst from my conscience
Looks like at 3:15 am
I made the executive decision

LOL

. . . .

108

To tell Logan everything I did
When we weren't together

My mouth feels like sandpaper
White fairy dust sprinkled on my dresser
The stranger—fuck! *Do I wake him?*
Think, think, think...
We were dancing at the bar
Went someplace more intimate
Came home, smoked a little weed
I rub my eyes and sigh
Light up a joint in the sweaty sun
My distractions have collateral damage
Can anyone tell I'm breaking?

emotional bleeding

A monster of self-doubt, cynicism

An *I hate everybody* teenage attitude

The house is a mess

Can't feel my heart in my chest

Days feel like weeks

No color in my cheeks

Laundry is like lifting weights

I become gray

There is no blue

When there is no blue

There is no me

Emotional bleeding

Depression is not a question

But an explanation of how

I should be farther along by now

I don't know why I'm made this way

They say

Every downfall is a new beginning

But I don't want to fall again

I just want to

Feel something

blood on my hands

The weight of his mistakes lies heavy on my shoulders
I hover over a beer bottle and white powder
Misogynistic frat boys and pick-me girls sing behind me
I close my eyes and feel the panic stir in my belly
My father's suicide threats are my fault
I shake the memory from my head
Take a drink of the emptiness in my cup

If I walk out of this hotel into the water
Would anyone care?

take you down

I'm a chameleon
With people I'm dating
No, I don't want your house
Your dog, your children
But you don't know this
Because I have you in my grip
I take you down
To the depths of my hips
And make you forget
Who you're making love with

the ravenel

My vision is flooded
Bottles scattered around worn red converse
My palms grip the railing so hard my fingers blister
I bang my forehead against the cement
And taste iron on my tongue

I can't take this pain anymore
Stare down a 180-foot drop
Scream through violent tears
Let me out
Let me out
Let me out
For the love of god
LET ME OUT
And wake up to my alarm

letters never sent VIII

FALL 2018

Dear B,

I placed us on the shelf and dove back into my reality: boys, booze, drugs, blackouts. At this point, my life was just something that happened to me—a show I watched from the back row, the cheap seats.

It was dusk when you facetimed me. Owls cried in the background, reminding me that the day was coming to an end. I could hear the nervousness and uncertainty in your voice. You were aimlessly driving around, a habit you had developed as soon as you got your license. You'd drive for hours, listening to the same five songs, trying to work through the noise in your head. "Burning gas", you called it.

My stomach was in my throat, and I was choking back tears when you told me. I knew this would be it. If you did this, the potential for North Carolina would be over. Through my screen, you looked like a wide-eyed, scared child. You were talking so fast, behaving as if the walls were closing in on you, and in many ways, they were.

I needed to save you to save us. You needed someone to come and take you away from everything for a little while. I told you to wait until I got home so we could talk in person. I tried to remain calm while my heart was pounding in my chest. I already had flights pulled up on my laptop. I felt anger at myself for my complacency in the last few months. Then, the anger at myself morphed into rage against you. How did we get here? How could you let this happen?

The thought of our future disintegrating drained the color from my cheeks. I knew if I didn't let my guard down now and tell you how much I loved you, I could lose you forever. I wanted your hand to hold mine so tightly that sand couldn't seep through. I wanted to remember what it felt like to hold you in the mornings, what you felt like on rainy spring days and cozy fall afternoons. I wanted your holidays, late-night pillow talks, and family party debriefs. I wanted to watch you brush your teeth in your boxers and feel you kiss me goodnight. I wanted a life with you. I've always wanted a life with you.

You're the one I'm supposed to be with—it's so clear, I can smell the ocean nearby. Maybe I didn't believe it before, but now I do. You will always be the person I come home to.

I will get through to you, B. You don't have to do this. We'll be together again, and all of this will feel trivial. A memory we look back on, laughing at the bullet we dodged. We'll tell the story of our love's obstacles, how we ran through haunted woods to be together. No more love triangle. It's our story, B, and it's worth fighting for.

My flight leaves on Thursday. Don't make any decisions before then. We'll be okay.

I love you. I am so dangerously in love with you.

M

who

Staring out airplane windows
Traveling to everyone else's lives,
Time whispers daily,
When will I build mine?

delicate hands

She sat on the piano
As he smoked his cigar
Hand up her dress, he said
I usually don't do this
His wife is the love of his life
Yet his mistress is the reason
He's still alive
One man with two faces
And the two women who love him

This man will live for decades
Holding two delicate hands
One in the morning
And one in the evening

doe-eyed

I have a terrible habit
Of believing someone
Who says something
That means nothing

....
120

letters never sent IX

FALL 2018

Dear B,

Tonight was the first time we were alone since the summer of 2015. I think I changed my outfit six times before you picked me up.

I was nervous to see you, B. It wasn't the familiar childlike excitement I usually experienced. There was too much at stake now. I had to play every card to make you feel safe enough to not go through with this. I know you say I change my mind too much, I only know how to leave, and I can't commit. But I was here. I was ready. I came home.

It was pouring rain as we drove through our town. Country music played softly on the radio. I didn't know where we were headed, and like always, it didn't matter. We had one night to comb through four years, to decide if we wanted to be together, to figure out how we could make that happen. In six months, I was moving back home. That was plenty of time for you to make room for me. You hated that you'd have to wait six months, and I hated that you couldn't find the patience.

....

We talked in circles for hours, without any resolution. Once we started drinking, I couldn't stop. I feared this would be the last time I saw you. The drunker I got, the sadder I became. Why wasn't I enough for you? Wasn't me moving back home proof for you? I didn't understand why she got to have the life we dreamed about so quickly.

We sat on the bed of your truck, sipped from a wine bottle, and stared into the woods. I had no idea what your decision would be. But when I told you how scared I was, you took my hand, played our song, and danced with me on that dirt road. I melted into your collarbone and tears streamed down my face. You smelled like my future, and I wanted to stay in that moment forever.

I'm certain you're going to be with me. Your family is going to understand. Your parents will still love you. Your friends will support you. My family will come around, eventually. After all this time, we're going to pick each other. It's time to play out our dream of North Carolina shores and curly-headed kids.

I won't sleep tonight. All I can do is hope you choose us. Hope you choose me.

M

just for tonight

Hold me down
With your hands
On my shoulders
Just for tonight
I don't want to float away

savior complex

Please
Step back from the ledge
Put your head on my chest
I'll kiss your forehead
And love you through this

bargaining

My heart melts inside my chest
It drips from my fingertips
My brain sends smoke
Through my eardrums
I am one-half broken
And one-half lost

Lying back on a used sofa
I'd do anything
To switch places with her

dusty concrete

I'm kneeling on dusty concrete
Sweat and dirt cover my face
I spit blood on the floor, *I'm still alive*
They've tied my arms behind my back
My bloody wrists ache with the chains
Remnants of a white dress barely cover my body
I laugh to the floor; *they don't know what I'm capable of*
A rat with more freedom scurries across my toes

And with every ounce of power
I scream again
LET ME OUT
LET ME OUT
LET ME OUT

evangeline

I'll wake with her in my bed
Her hot breath on my neck
3:33 am, the best timing
She'll lean over to kiss me
Slip her fingers into my
Heart and light me up
Sending me into daydreams
Making me believe
I can conquer anything

plum blossum

I was never what you wanted
Or what you needed
But I hope my words stay with you
When I couldn't

I hope she gives you all the things
That I wouldn't

judas

Drag my memory

To the trash bin

Pull every strand

Of blonde hair

Off your shirt

Shower a million hours

To get my body

Off of yours

Wipe my smell

From your nose

Cleanse your ears

Of my voice

Scrape my name

Off your tongue

Till I become

No one

nursery rhyme

In love at nineteen

With nothing in between

No idea where to start

Settling wouldn't be smart

So we swipe and match

Three dates then detach

Nervous and sober

Oh, no, no

We'll have the cab—wait, do you want merlot?

Till our lips are stained a subtle pink

And we don't have time to rethink

Gain the confidence to caress their skin

But love can't grow in a bottle of gin

Let's close out—we know that line well

Convince ourselves we finally fell

Race to the bedroom, close the door

Relieved this one doesn't feel like a chore

LET ME OUT

Morning will come and we're still strangers
Ashamed, thinking this was a no-brainer
Sneak out the door before they wake
Why does this all seem so fucking fake?

letters never sent X

FALL 2018

Dear B,

This will be the last letter I write to you. This is the last time you will come close to my life. I can't believe I ever believed anything you told me. You were never going to leave her. I was just some fantasy you clung to as a break from your boring life. You couldn't even look me in the eyes when you told me. You stared at the road while I cried in the passenger seat. Ten years of back and forth and I was ready to finally be together. I put my pride down. I chose you. I chose us.

You'll be miserable for the rest of your life. You don't love her, you don't love me, you don't love yourself, and I will not be damaged in the refusal to choose your own life.

I slammed your car door shut. I hoped I broke something in that stupid truck. I'm blocking your number. You'll never be able to get in touch with me. I'm a ghost to you.

. . . .

Honestly, I'm happy this is over. I'm happy one of us was able to be so stupid that it forced us to end things. I'm telling you right now, I'm going to have a great life. I'll find someone who adores me, loves me, and cherishes me. And you'll have to live with that for the rest of your life. You said for the last ten years, you've wanted to marry me. Well, I hope you enjoy watching me marry someone else.

I hope you're happy with your decision, B, because there's no other option anymore. No more North Carolina. You've chosen your reality, and I'm getting as far away from it as possible.

M

lose my mind

To pass the time
I'll lose my mind
Walk down hallways
Rip holes in lingerie
Take a baseball bat
To picture frames
Pour cement on my skin
Call up Amy Winehouse,
Health Ledger, and Kurt Cobain
Ask them what it's like
Up in heaven

brainwash

I scroll
Till my eyes roll
Into the back of my head
And I want to change
Just about everything

I stand in front of mirrors
Gripping my thighs
Pinching my belly
Twisting curls

Count the squares
On the ceiling
Comparison feels
Like a game
I'll never win

disorganized

I'm anxious
And avoidant
I want you
But at a distance
I'm unsettled
When you're close
I'm obsessed
When you leave
Come back
And I feel better
Stay long
I retreat
I want you
I need you
Come back
Hold me
Love me
I don't want you
I can't do this
Don't come back
Let go of me

claustrophobic

I've known this type of hole
Like I'm entirely on my own
Though I have someone to hold

I lie restless on this mattress
And feel their back against my bare chest
Not knowing how long I can take this

I don't understand contentment
I cannot resist resentment
Toward a person I believe
I can't spend my life with

rhododendron

My head feels as heavy as a loaded gun
I'm ashamed of what I've done
And what I've forgotten
How do you know when a habit becomes a problem?

I touch the girl in the mirror
My hair is broken and brassy
Teeth are see-through and yellow
Under-eye bags have bags
(I could sleep inside of them, if I slept)
My face is puffy and red
A combination of consumption
I'm bloated as if someone
Pumped me full of hot air

Life is long and I can't be here
I'm not excited about tomorrow
Not next month or next year
Not the same pulsating music
Or the same validation

....

Given a million different ways
While the plot stays the same

Iron bones fill my throat
I throw up in the sink

I am just like him

I knew I was in hell
When I realized I'd become
Everything I'd been running from

what is wrong with you?

In the last few months
I've started a business
Booked a couple of trips
Fallen in love with someone I don't know yet
He's perfect, might be *the one*
I'm already sending him rings
He buys everything like he's rockstar rich
We have lots of sex, never fight
He's almost godlike, like me

I'm going to become Instagram famous
You should see these comments
It's about time people look to me for advice
I'm successful, smart, funny, borderline perfect
I mean, look at me—look at my life
Work out six days a week
Only eat between twelve and three
My body is tight like leather

And my clothes are chic
I'm at the top of my game

Then suddenly, something
Comes blazing in
Pinches my rainbow flame
Where did all my colors go?
Where did all the people go?
My skin transforms to gray
Dark circles surround my eyes
My hair is unwashed, unkept
I want to sleep for the next six weeks
Embarrassment floods my veins
Don't get why this happens
Who pinched my rainbow flame?

brian

I can draw your shoulder tattoo

Perfectly on paper

Each morning I wake up

And trace it with my finger

missed calls

It's coming back again

Eighty-foot wave

Can't swim fast enough

Water fills my lungs

I'm

Going

Under

rotting out my teeth

Perhaps I don't have a personality

This fire in my belly, storm in my chest

Are just reactions, responses, triggers

Did everyone else get instructions to life?

Even if I did, I wouldn't read them

Most days I don't listen, and even when I do

I can't decipher what's real and what's fake

The voices in my head are sweet candy, persuasive

Or sour, rotting out my teeth

The bad guys look like good guys and the good guys look like bad guys

I can't trust this stranger in the mirror

The woman reflected is faceless, worn

Like a tired housewife who chose the wrong partner

An abandoned statue that no one cares to visit

I don't know who I am without my insanity

Maybe I don't care to

I don't think I've met myself yet

bedside begging

Dear God (if there is a God)
Send me a man to rely on
Pockets to survive on
Woman's touch to lean on
Friends I can call on
A heart that beats on its own
Maybe a house to call home

I'm not winning the war against myself
My brain is disintegrating by the minute
I'm losing control
And I can't go on like this anymore

periwinkle

It's a long road, baby
Holes in shoes
Bloody feet
Salty sweat

My head hits a pillow
That isn't mine
Isn't yours
Isn't ours

Darkness falls
On this highway
And I'll scream your name
Through unfamiliar streets

Nobody will hear me
Because nobody knows me

letters never sent XI

SUMMER 2019

Dear B,

It's been almost a year since we spoke. You've been trying to reach out to me since that day I slammed your truck door, and I never answer. I don't care what you have to say. Even though I'm clinging to anger with all my strength, I still know I'm supposed to be yours, and you're supposed to be mine.

I guess I've felt this whisper of worthlessness my entire life. I mean, my own father couldn't bear to stick around—how could I expect anyone else to? I've been beaten down to the core. Not just with us, but with everything in my life. There are too many parts of me you haven't met. I feel like I've walked into this world cursed. I don't have much energy. I think about leaving this world often. But I won't tell you this; I couldn't. It was my business, and I was taking care of it, poorly. I think I'm just one of those people who don't deserve to be happy.

Yesterday, you showed up on my doorstep wearing a red t-shirt and god-awful cargo pants. You'd been working outside all summer, so your cheeks were sun-kissed, and your arms were golden brown. Even though I was filled with resentment, I still wanted to make out with you. Unconditional love is annoying like that. I wished you'd just forget me as hard as I try to forget you. But that wish is fleeting because I loved how you never let me forget you.

It's been three months since I moved back home, and I'm as miserable as ever. I'm a mile away from the life you made with someone else. I watch it unfold every time I get on the highway. I poured a drink when I saw your truck roll down the driveway. Whatever you had to say, I knew I couldn't be sober for it. I can't be sober for most things, most days.

I've had the house to myself a lot this summer, and there has been a revolving door of boys I never got with in high school. I secretly hoped you'd hear how well I was doing without you. Or who I was doing without you. I wanted you to think I moved on.

You were sitting quietly at my mother's island, the one she designed herself. This was the first home she built without my father, a testament to her newfound independence. Even though I won't admit it, I'm so happy she never moved out of our town.

I offered you a drink, but you declined. I felt awkward and uncomfortable. I sat there quietly, waiting for you to speak.

....

There was a pause that lasted a lifetime, then you started pouring your heart out. You just got back from your brother's wedding and had a dream about us the night before.

"Meg, the dream it was so real. We were walking through the fields. You had a sundress on. It was summer and I was teasing you, making you laugh. We kept hugging, kissing, and laughing. The sun was setting. I woke up so happy because I thought we were together again. And then, I had to watch my brother get married, thinking about you the entire time. Thinking what you would look like walking down the aisle. I want to marry you. I've always wanted to marry you, Meg. Once we got back, I had to come see you. I'm so sorry, please."

I sipped my drink through your monologue, overwhelmed with your comfortability in my home.

The way you looked when telling me about this dream, it was so, what is the word? Innocent. Your eyes change when you're excited, there is a lot of blinking. You have these doe eyes that are tragically kind. You put your hands on your face multiple times and scratch your facial hair. I could tell you're tired, that you've been ruminating on this for days. I'm sure you burnt gas for hours until you gained the courage to come over. You fiddled with your hat, turning it front to back to front again. You have never been able to sit still.

"I'll blow my life up tomorrow if you promise to be all in with me. If you promise to build your life with me. You are the best thing that has ever been mine, Meg. I'm here. I know we are supposed to be together. Let's do this." For hours, you pleaded with a girl you used to know. If you only knew how unreachable I was.

My belly became warm, and my eyes went glossy. When we were finished combing through possible solutions, we sat there in silence. You waited. I tried to filter through my options. I thought, "no matter what this boy does, I will always love him. Of course, I want to marry him. This is my soulmate; I've loved him since I was twelve years old. And he's here, waiting for me. He's been trying to come back to me since I left. Even though he's panting, dirty, and late, he came back for me. I can do this with him. It's not perfect, it's messy, and complicated, but he's the one. It has always been him. I can have a life with B."

Then, without control or warning, I retreated. I started speaking without thinking, and let flames roll off my tongue, "This is exactly what I needed to hear months ago, fuck, even four years ago. You have an entire life with someone else!" I slammed my hand on the counter. "You can't show up like this. Are you kidding me?" I felt the tears well up in my eyes; I was not going to let you see me cry. I don't let anyone see me cry. "It wasn't supposed to be this way. You have no idea what you want." Really, it was me who didn't know what she wanted.

My cheeks turned red, "We don't even know what we look like in the mornings, how we like our coffee, if we could survive one single fight. Do you use an electric or regular toothbrush? What if you hate the way I eat chips? Or get makeup everywhere? I'd be a terrible wife. Oh my god, awful. I'm so messy and I can't keep anything clean. I lose everything. I've never been able to commit to anything, I mean look at us!"

You knew I was going to keep going, so you didn't speak. I scoffed, "My family will hate this, you know? Your parents have no idea who I am anymore. They'll think you're insane. They'll hate me." I looked down at my feet, not looking at you once.

I shook my head to reassure my decision, "Nope. I am leaving as soon as I can save enough money to get the FUCK out of here." I put my head in my hands, feeling so exhausted by my entire life. I wanted to dive into your arms but too much history stood between us. I paused and calmly said, "This town is a trap. You're telling me this too late." I swallowed and prepared for what I was about to say next, "I don't want this anymore." Shocked myself for how easily I can lie.

I met your gaze, you didn't look innocent anymore. You looked embarrassed, like I just gave you a test that you did not pass. Red ink all over our love story.

B, I'm no longer the bright-eyed teenage girl in red Converse, ready to take on the world. I'm not the country-loving small-town girl in a sundress. I'm no longer goofy and ridiculous, the type of person who knows how to make you laugh. I'm not the class clown or homecoming queen. I'm not kind or gentle—I'm ugly, mean. I hate myself. I'm an after picture. Used up and tired. I'm exactly what everyone expected I'd be: broken.

After we hugged goodbye, for the last time, I drank myself to sleep.

I'm sorry you'll never be enough for me to stay.

M

pour out

I wish to open this bottle

Pour out loneliness, shame, and regret

Fill rivers with lost vulnerability

Give you space

Set you free

And let you out

fire away

I sip tequila on the rocks, ice stings my lips,
And puff a cigarette into the winter sky.
How am I going to replace the stolen parts of me?
Which mess belongs to who?

Pieces of me are scattered along the East Coast
Everyone's life started, mine stands still
The loss of my father, my family
Memory drifts to our dinner table
Five of us talking about our safe lives
A science project on the counter
Ice cream cake in the freezer
It is all love and laughter
When they start to disappear
Slowly, then all at once
My dinner turns cold, moldy
But I'm still so hungry
No one to talk to
But empty seats
And now I'm expected to

....

Get it together, grow up,
Keep it to yourself, or *let it go*
But how can I move on,
When this is how my life started?

21 summer

My head nestles into your chest

I hear crickets to my left

I start to cry

You pull up my chin, wipe my cheek

You have blood in your veins, a beating heart

A gap between your teeth

But you're pulling away from me

You're melting into the trees

Now I'm alone in this lucid dream

Falling to my knees

I sit there until morning, waiting

This was never the way it was meant to be

You were supposed to choose me

the choices we make

If I knew leaving you that summer night
Would be the worst mistake of my life
I'd unpack my suitcase, call the whole thing off
Race to your house, tap on your window
Tell you I'm staying, make a new plan
Because a life without you was never an option

3:23 AM

I take a drag while I fantasize about my funeral:
I never saw it coming.
She was so happy.
Funny girl, always making people laugh.
People say the nicest things about the dead.
Sigh into my phone—no messages.
Pull on the cigarette, shake the thoughts from my head.
I don't know how to fix this,
But I'll be damned if this is how I end.

chosen family

They placed food on my desk when I couldn't eat
Held my hand when I couldn't see straight
Danced in the living room when I found the energy
Pulled my hair back as I threw up on the street

Texted my boyfriends when I couldn't explain
Filled rooms with people to celebrate my birthdays
Laughed at my jokes, said I was going places
MJ you are meant for microphones and stages

They held my head above water
Running from a broken home, this was my shelter
Handed his letters from jail with no judgement
Another one arrived, let me know if you want it

Poured my drinks out when I had enough
Talked with me till the sun came up
Forced hugs when I joked, *no physical touch!*
Laid next to me, when I couldn't get up

LET ME OUT

Put me in the car, rolled the windows down, to drive in silence

Even on my worst days, they could tell I was trying

I would've never made it to my next chapter,

Without Nancy, Lanie, Talia, Betty, or Vanessa

III

We Could Not Predict This

....

"Memories are immortal. They're deathless and precise. They have the power of giving you joy and perspective in hard times. Or, they can strangle you. Define you in a way that's based more in other people's tucked-up perceptions than truth."

—Viola Davis, *Finding Me*

the escape

My red Converse crunch gravel
I cling tightly to a busted briefcase
Without a second thought or stop
Rushing cars vibrate my core
Some people don't have patience
For a young girl growing up
It's a blessing and a curse to be invisible

I have no money but I'm not poor
The richest person in the room
Is the one with the most freedom
I will play with the cards I've been dealt
Okay with losing until I win
Don't know where I'm going
Don't have a plan
I'm a lonely, rambling man
But I will find something

And with my last dusty pen
I'll rewrite my ending

carnations

Depression goes through my phone to make sure happiness stopped calling. Everyone either hates me or has given up on me. I'm a skyscraper of trauma that sits in the center of a ghost town. I'll never be as important as I want to be. I could sleep for six weeks and still be tired. I could drink the ocean dry and still be thirsty. I could be surrounded by people who truly love me and still feel lonely.

naked

I can't tell you
I've been on fire
For most of my life
And the people who were supposed
To love me the most
Didn't notice the burns

I can't tell you
Abandonment sinks its teeth into my shoulder
Peels down the skin of my back
And makes me crawl out

I can't tell you
Art and music are the only ways
I can make sense of all the pain
Without them, I would die

I can't tell you
I'm terrified if you know
How my blood flows

You will put your hands up
Say, *this is too much for me*
And I will be alone
Again

hubris

I am self-righteous, like a king who finds himself wronged
I post Instagram essays, not captions
As if I'm not the most uneducated educated human you could meet
It's obvious I am losing my mind

Giving herself up too early is the earliest lesson a young girl learns
If I met my ego, I'd grab the sword from my waist
Plunge a dagger into the center of its power
And watch it bleed out
No regrets, no remorse

My commitments are hurricanes that last a few days
My promises are a bratty teenager's room—unkept
I'm a laughingstock to the townspeople in my head
Who stone each creative idea to death
As I tame my brain to sleep, they laugh outside my window

I am the mistakes of my father
And the disintegrated dreams of my mother
I run in circles like flames are chasing me

....

LET ME OUT

My melancholic ways are laced with cocaine
If unregulated emotions were a billboard, I'd be on it

My lips are paper thin and pale
My nose is a centerpiece for a family of six
But I'm at a table of one
If I had all the money in the world, I'd choose vanity

I have the audacity to think someone would read this
I am no one, I am nothing, I am not worthy
If I ever made history, my story would be
She tried at everything and didn't finish anything
Not even this po—

shane

I need your familiar voice

I want to curl up on your chest

Laugh about the past

Mourn what could've been

Accept what we are

I want your playful showers

Bubble-bath talks

Songs that remind you of me

I want your heartbreak

Not your friendship

You don't know this

And I won't tell you

iris

I panic so easily

Can't love peacefully

Convinced you'll abandon me

gone mad

I step on bottlecaps

Till my heels bleed and I lose feeling.

Sweat slips down my forehead.

I laugh hysterically.

My ribs peek out of my torso

As if I could dip my bloody fingers inside,

Pull one out, and screech *Try me!*

My knees melt into pieces of salt.

Add more, push harder, pull faster,

Gulp down poison like water.

You think THIS is torture?

I laugh a deranged laugh.

More! More! More!

Is this all you got?

IS THIS ALL YOU GOT?

A slap hits my cheek.

The earth fills my teeth.

I smile a dirty, toothy grin.

They tear open my white dress.

....

Cuts, bruises, gashes—
This woman is broken!
Bumping elbows, nodding, wicked snarling,
They toss their greasy heads back.
I sit there for a moment
Naked,
Waiting.

They think they have the upper hand,
They don't know this type of crazy
Always wins.

turn the faucet on

Drain them
From my hips
Forgive myself
For all the times
I was conquered
Instead of worshiped

pediatrician

We go to those with credentials
Tell them we're not living our potential

So they take out a little white paper
Klonopin, Xanax, Ativan
What's your flavor?

Don't drink or you'll fall to the floor
And don't forget your co-pay at the door

....
176

collection of confessions

Hid behind the couch for most of my life,
No energy in me to stand up and fight.
Desperate for someone's permission,
I got it from a man named Addiction.
The love felt real but it was actually evil,
Ten years of my life spent dancing with the devil.
Locked in a cage, an inmate in prison,
Now I'm stuck with this chronic condition.

The breakup was long; no one played clean.
Many mornings hunched over a toilet seat,
Sweating and shaking, back against the wall,
Whispering, *This is the last wake-up call.*
And each time I meant it, I really did,
Until all those justifications rolled in:
You're still young. You're sowing your oats.
Use the credit card—you're not actually broke.

One day I found it in me to say goodbye.
We both stared at each other and cried
He didn't take it well, never thought I'd quit,

....

Expected a more long-term relationship.

And I haven't seen him since; I'm three years sober

Proudly wearing a scarlet letter on my shoulder.

It'll be okay; he won't touch me again.

First time in my life I'm unafraid to be human.

harbor

One day
I'll show compassion
For when I fell off the boat
And you kept driving

freedom

Where do I go
When there's nowhere to go?
When an exhale
Could blow me away?
Two years
Circling the airport—
Life's hard
When I'm the runaway.
Indecisiveness,
Fear of commitment
Leave me
Wandering—
No, frozen.
Am I supposed to be here?
Or here?
Or here?
Pavement stings my feet.
What am I running from now?
Never fight, always flight.

Where do I go,

When there's everywhere to go?

Achingly lonely

But beautifully free.

sleepless in seattle

You were heartbroken

I was floating

Cold sheets

Twisted melodies

Blinked through darkness

Bargained with the sun

Please stay down

I'm sorry, I'm a mess

Darling, you have no idea

community pool

I know how to swim
But I sat there on a blanket
Frozen with a cigarette
Watching people who didn't know anything
Dive right in

reasons

Loving me feels like solving an impossible problem.

I drown us both in my imagination. Our lungs fill up with *Who is she? Who were you with?* We're forced to swallow *Do you even love me? Do you even care? Are you even listening? You don't do anything for me.*

After years of surviving on small patches of air, you'll realize you don't have to be underwater with me. You don't need to spend your life gasping for chances to speak. Your ankles aren't chained to my ocean floor. Eventually, you'll let go.

Then I'll drift, with my hair swaying in the current of lost love. I'll gladly return home, float down until I feel the earth underneath my fingernails.

If there is one thing I know, love is not meant for a woman like me.

sobriety

I'm buried under
Pages of
Self-help
Self-worth
Self-love
Self-trust
Let me
Formally introduce
Myself to me

At twenty-three
In this 9-to-5, forty-hour week
I'm learning to treat myself kindly
To not retreat
To not take the backseat
This time, I won't leave
This is where I want to be

But today
I don't want to read

....

I canceled therapy
My eyelids are heavy

Pull down the shades
I'm going back to sleep

who is this person

19

I am slipping

Somebody listen

How is this happening to me?

23

Writing on walls

In my own language

Even I don't understand it

humarock

3,000 miles away

Watching the sun set on a new city

I heard you're still unhappy

And that always kills me

Because when summer comes around the corner

I think of our life if you had left her

paper rings

I trace my ring finger with my thumb

And think to myself

He can't put forever on a runner

Even if I tried to be his everything

He wanted this one thing

It's a lesson I keep learning

When it comes to love

Timing is everything

word

just love me the way I am

When will you believe me?

I'm not speaking in tongues or going crazy.

I'm not messy, delusional, or different.

I have more control than you.

You know me at my worst but look away at my best.

I have the agency to create my reality—

It's not yours to design for me.

Your comfort is my purgatory.

Should I cover myself in rubies and jewels,

Sign autographs, live under a spotlight?

If I were a voice people listened to,

A face people related to,

A story people clung to,

Would you finally say it?

I believe you.

I believe in you.

forget-me-not

It does not matter
Who listens, follows,
Unfollows, points,
Laughs

This does not belong
In the cracks
Of your soul

This is meant
For blank canvases
Lined pages
New melodies

A soul in pieces
Demands to be art

boat man

Boat man stood six feet tall
Ice-blue eyes that could leave frost on your hands
A side smile missing a cigarette, though he hated smokers
A retired cool kid, backwards hat
The kind of man pre-therapy me would obsess over
Who post-therapy me found, surfaced
His skin looked like summer though we lived in Seattle
And I didn't see him in the winter

Boat man's features were chiseled, godlike
He told me one night he loved me physically
But not emotionally
And before I could agree
He said *sorry* repeatedly
As if I was already in love

We went on fake dates
Every three or four months
He'd pretend to listen to my stories
(He was awful at pretending)

....

LET ME OUT

He thought it wasn't polite
To get naked immediately
He talked about himself a lot
And about sports—so many sports
I'd let my mind drift while he spoke
Waiting for him to get to the point
So we could go back to his waterfront home
And make love for exactly thirty minutes
Boat man's house was spotless
Staged, like the rest of him

The way he had sex was organized yet provocative
Right, left, moan, smack, dig, thrust, thrust, thrust
Grind, pulse, suck, lick, grab, tug, thrust, slap
Nice ass, so hot, sexy body, just like that, yeah, yeah, yeah
The sex only emotionally unavailable men can give you

One night, after he finished and I didn't
He confessed, *I don't understand how I'm not married*
(Once men turn thirty-five, it's like they never knew about timing)
He listed off credentials like a rehearsed sales pitch
I'm tall, good-looking, house, boat, nice family
What do you think?

I pretended to care
Thinking to myself
He's the loneliest human on the planet   LoL

....

193

walking away

I don't know what love is
But I know what love isn't
Maybe that will be enough

♡

the escape

My red Converse crunch gravel
I cling tightly to a busted briefcase
Without a second thought or stop
Rushing cars vibrate my core
Some people don't have patience
For a young girl growing up
It's a blessing and a curse to be invisible

I have no money but I'm not poor
The richest person in the room
Is the one with the most freedom
I will play with the cards I've been dealt
Okay with losing until I win
Don't know where I'm going
Don't have a plan
I'm a lonely, rambling man
But I will find something

And with my last dusty pen
I'll rewrite my ending

Fuckyea M!

....

carnations

Depression goes through my phone to make sure happiness
stopped calling. Everyone either hates me or has given up on
me. I'm a skyscraper of trauma that sits in the center of a ghost
town. I'll never be as important as I want to be. I could sleep for
six weeks and still be tired. I could drink the ocean dry and still
be thirsty. I could be surrounded by people who truly love me
and still feel lonely.

calendulas

There are three types of loneliness.

One: The type you feel when you can't help someone who won't help themselves. Watching someone turn sour. Losing someone who is right in front of you.

Two: The type you feel in your bones. No one to hold at night, no friends to call on, no family. Days go by without a text. Life feels long, this thing you didn't commit to but must go through. It sets you on fire from the toes up, forcing to watch yourself burn.

Three: The type with no explanation or warning. That feeling you get when you're alone in a crowded room. Misunderstood even when they understand you. Tired eyes, melancholy responses, and do-not-disturb notifications. It's the type of loneliness that turns you into a shadow, a ghost. No one can stop you from disappearing.

letters never sent XII

MARCH 2022

Dear B,

Did you ever wonder what our lives would look like if we ended up together? Did you ever wonder where I went?

When I left Massachusetts, I was newly sober and resentful. When my car left the driveway, again, I promised myself that I would never come back. The only possible solution my youthful brain could comprehend was to erase my entire existence, push away old friends, and pretend like my past didn't exist. When you're in the eye of the storm it's nearly impossible to see resolution. At the time, if someone offered me an entirely new life, I would've taken it without hesitation.

The thought of my younger self wanting to be another human being makes me wince. There was so much good underneath all the mess, B. I took it for granted. But that is what happens when you hate yourself; it's too easy to hate everything around you too.

....

About a month ago, I moved into my second apartment in Seattle. It was a basement unit with a tiny backyard. It wasn't anything special, but I was happy I could plant flowers while living in the city. I hate apartment living, I wish I could walk outside and put my feet in the grass.

In the middle of moving, your memory flashed through my brain, and I couldn't breathe. Sober thoughts are wild like that, forcing you to pause at any given moment. Sobriety never cares how important your to-do lists are, ignoring things is a luxury I cannot afford anymore. The following night, I had a dream that you somehow found me in this hole in the wall, 3000 miles away.

The dream was extremely clear: as I swung open my door, I met your doe-eyes in pure shock. My jaw hit the floor, I squealed as if I opened a present I had been waiting for, and jumped into your arms. Our embrace felt like we were reunited after a long, arduous war. You looked like a man; strong with calloused hands. You stepped into my place with familiarity and gave me a "this is where you live?" type of look. You frowned when you noticed my life was wrapped up in four little boxes. It was as if you felt guilty for not arriving sooner.

I didn't understand why I'd be thinking about you so vividly; however, I knew there was a reason. But like a sickness you refuse to go to the doctor for, I never acted on it. I waited, and now I am choking on the consequences. I'm drowning in my own regrets. I cannot breathe. Why didn't I put my pride aside and reach out?

....

I didn't know much about women's intuition yet, but B, I know a lot about it now.

Maybe it's my ego or a savior complex, but I think I could've saved you. I could've bought us a ticket to anywhere. If you had told me how you were feeling, I could've flown home. I would've moved home. Why did I never ask you to come with me? Why didn't I tell you what I was going through? Why didn't I tell you I loved you to your face? Why didn't I check in on you? When did I stop writing you letters? Why did I keep leaving you behind? Why did I think I was better than everyone? I didn't know you were hurting. I forced myself to move on. I thought you had found some peace. But the truth was, I didn't have the full story. I never did.

From the depths of my soul, I am so incredibly sorry.

If we met today, our reckless youth wouldn't be able to separate us anymore. I could've been your safe space, that person who made 5 am a little more bearable. The person who gave you options. I would've asked you, "What do you want?" Even if the answer didn't include me. If you had been able to let yourself out of the life you never wanted, that would've been enough.

But if it was me, I would've found it in myself to commit to you. I'd anchor to the life I've wanted since I was little. We could've had the cutest relationship, B. I know it's been a lifetime of running away from home, but I'm so tired of running. I would've come back. I wanted to come back. You didn't know this. I never told you how I really felt about you.

I would've held your hand through life's blessings and tragedies. There would've been no need to chase, to hustle, to become something we weren't. We would've kept each other balanced, healthy. And if we didn't achieve a damn thing in this world, it wouldn't have mattered because we'd have each other.

Our life would've been too full and precious to play with. You'd make it to ninety-nine, B. You would've been surrounded by our family and a bunch of grandkids that loved you. I would've passed away shortly after because life on earth would've been unbearable. Life on earth without you is unbearable.

If I had done something, anything, maybe I wouldn't be standing in the back of this church. The organ wouldn't be playing, your brother wouldn't be speaking, and I wouldn't be stomaching your eulogy.

Who were you running from B?

What happened since I saw you last?

When did you start giving up?

Where were you trying to escape to?

Why were you being so reckless with your life?

How could you leave us like this?

M

white lilies

I would sell my soul

For one more

Conversation

Kiss

Hug

Laugh

Joint

Car ride

Phone call

I'd pool all my money

Drain my savings

Sell my belongings

Steal anything

To hear the rhythm

Of your heartbeat

I'd get on my knees

Place my forehead

To the pavement

Scream your name

In these streets

Till my lungs felt like fire

And my voice became weak

Praying to anything

That would listen

To make you come home

Come back

To me

To us

To your family

Please

I'll do anything

Now months

Are flying by

Sobbing into darkness

Because our world

Doesn't turn on its axis

Without you in it

I would rather

Feel everything and let it kill me
Than feel nothing at all

orchid

I'm a walking corpse in a sea full of
Happy people who lead happy lives
I don't know what happiness looks like
Without you anymore

Sometimes I dream of the spirit side
My head in the curve of your neck
Your scent, your laugh
We live on stars, sleep on planets
Achieve everything we never could
On earth

Honey, I want to die
For another chance at life
With you

longing

I dream of the day
I'll be safe in your arms
And we'll laugh to think
There was ever a life
Without each other

3:33 AM

My life could've turned out so differently. The least I could've done was make him stay a little longer. Even if it was for just one more year, one more month. I had so much left to say. What a tragic unfinished book we were.

So much of my life has been lived by other people's experiences and expectations. What would my life look like if I chose another path? If I stayed? All I want to do is go home. All I've ever wanted to do was go home.

I need to believe in reason behind all of this. I didn't walk away from my life over and over and over again just to be let down. Just to be alone.

God, if there is a God, please make this pain worth something. Please make me feel like I am on my way to a life greater than I can even imagine. I need to know I made the right choice.

And if not, I don't want to be here anymore.

they know (a folk song)

This plane is heading to a land
I've been calling home
Yet the people feel like mirrors
Reflections I don't know
And they know, they know

I'm sleeping next to him
He's the opposite of others
The ones who tore my feathers
I told him it's forever
But I know

I've been broken and deceived
Felt the shame twirl in my sheets
I want a love that is deceased
And the one thing I know
Is I cannot go back home
They know, they know

I brag about a brand-new coast

Where life is so damn clear

But lately I've been thinking

I chose quiet out of fear

And they know

I forgot who I was dancing for

These people know me to my core

What happens behind closed doors

Doesn't stay behind closed doors

Yeah, they've known

I've been broken and deceived

Felt the shame twirl in my sheets

I want a love that is deceased

And the only thing I know

Is I cannot go back home

They know, they know

It's close to closing time

Been waiting for the card decline

A purchase of a new life I thought

Would leave my past behind

But it won't

And they've known

....

LET ME OUT

I've been broken and deceived
Felt the shame twirl in my sheets
I want a love that is deceased
And the only thing I know
Is I want to go back home
This I know, this they've known

chamomile

It's that sweet spot in summer
When people around the world
Fall in love at the same time

In my head
I'm holding his hand
A band is playing
Songs we make love to

He slips his hand up my sundress
I feel the warmth of his skin
We're forehead to forehead
Kissing in a crowd of new beginnings

charleston

I don't miss drinking the way you'd think an addict would
The temptation doesn't come with an unrelenting need
Or the urge to water myself down so I can feel free
To black out years of my life
As if I could delete selected chapters and characters
My hands don't shake, my mouth doesn't water
I'm at peace with sobriety
A bed I will lie in for the rest of my life

I don't miss drinking the way you'd think an addict would
Months go by without a single thought of breaking
I don't avoid bars, clubs, or parties
A table of drunk people only annoys me
Like a mother with tiny children
Not once wanting to trade places

I miss drinking the way you miss an old friend
The one who shares your wildest memories
Like a dusty vault of your latest nights
And incredible, timeless stories

....

I miss drinking the way you miss an old lover

Who took up all your nights and weekends like oxygen

Surrounding you with people at all hours of the night

Party culture is a twenty-four-hour business

With a slogan of *community*

And you never realize you can breathe on your own

I miss drinking the way you miss a best friend

The one who never let you stay home

Alone

lessons unlearned

I believe I was sent into this life to learn a recurring lesson: you can't help someone who won't help themselves.

I spent my childhood trying to get my father sober. I believed I could be the one to save him. I thought that with enough letters, caretaking, and bargaining, I could make him realize I could make my dad come back to me. Not helping him felt like giving up, like I'd failed. I thought if he ended his life, it would be my fault. I put him on my tiny back and held him there until my knees broke and I started to get sick with him. I couldn't help someone who wouldn't help themselves.

Now, when I look at this new person, I can't breathe. Their depression fills the room. I feel them slipping away. I see them search outside themselves for relief. I see their reluctance to ask for help. I see myself start to tug, then pull, then push, then shove.

Here are ten solutions to one problem. Let's figure out how to get you better. I can make you feel better. I can make you feel okay again. Why won't you let me save you?

Then, when the lights go off in my room, I feel the familiar loneliness of trying to save someone who needs to save themselves. I feel that hollow responsibility I never asked for, but now consumes every thought: *If something happened to them, it would be my fault. If I don't step in and give my all to their problems, what does that say about me as a daughter, a friend, a partner, a sibling?*

You can't help someone who won't help themselves.

old school

I want an old-school kind of love.
A radio-on-their-shoulder-outside-your-window type of love.
The write-your-number-on-this-napkin, call-you-at-lunchtime,
This-song-reminded-me-of-you type of love.
The pick-you-up-at-8-o'clock-just-to-drive love.
Flowers-on-your-doorstep, rose-petals-in-the-bathtub,
You're-the-most-beautiful-woman-I've-ever-seen love.
An old-school kind of love.

The type of love that makes you feel seen
In a world that wants you invisible,
As if this person was designed for you to fall into
Like a warm bed after a long day.
Wipe-tears-when-you're-sad, hold-your-hand-when-you're-scared,
Celebrate-your-Sundays kind of love.
A love that feels like a fire you make love in front of,
When the clocks turn back and it's dark at 4 pm.
An old-school kind of love
Drenched in loyalty

Where faithfulness is never questioned,

Bonds are never broken,

And forever is the only possible outcome.

influencer

I'm in between a screen and the window.
Someone closed it; I was just taking a minute,
Had to delete it for a second.
It's loud inside:
Girls screaming, people dancing,
Succeeding, crying, laughing.

I'm so bored of it—
The Amazon lists, the likes, the clicks,
The oversized lips, influencer tips.
Hey, look at this!
I made a million last week
And I'm only seventeen!
Ew, you work 9-to-5?
That is so 2015.
This is the NEW
American dream.
Get ready with me!

Constantly posting—
If you don't record it,
Did it happen?
How can we be creative
When our brains are overcrowded
With everyone's opinions
I guess if you can't beat 'em,
Join 'em?

secrets bond

Tonight, I'm cursing my newfound life
My perspective's 45 percent bullshit
For every hero in a story there's a villain
And tonight, I will be Lilith
I'll pour this mocktail down the sink
Paint my lips red, draw circles around my eyes
Peel whiskey off the shelf and drink until I can't think
I want to self-destruct for one last night
Before I return to the numbness of a settled life

Our parents helped us with the house
We don't have a wedding date yet
I just bought this new car
When are you heading home for the holidays?
When are you taking the vacation?
Are adult conversations just updates?

I'm bored of all of it
I want to dance till my limbs are achy and sore
In a dress that's too small for my chest

....

LET ME OUT

I want to have sweaty sex with a stranger
And never talk to them again

Secrets bond better than banter
So tell me something I can dip my hands into
Tell me about your dirtiest sex, forbidden love
I'll listen as the warm fluid courses through my body
And the opinions of my family flow away
Let's do something we can't tell anyone
Wake up in the morning asking *What did we do last night?*

Give me a break from the vacuuming, the cleaning
meetings, bills, the same restaurants
The same sex, the same people
Let me into a world that sparkles and shines
Please, keep me up all night

I didn't fight my way through hell
To become this boring version of myself

....
221

just because

You don't understand
Doesn't mean I have to explain

eternal

Most things aren't meant to be forever. Life's not secure, comfortable, or eternal. Contentment is an illusion. It's boredom dressed up as stability, unraveling itself as time goes on. Playing it safe is a useless battle against the only guarantee in this life: change.

pitt street

I miss the belly laughs

Sitting around a table, still drunk from the day before

I miss letting my hair down

The community of debauchery

You did what? and *You slept with him?*

Heart-to-hearts that reveal true feeling

And the drama—so much drama

I miss the spontaneity of a road trip, a risky text

A date with a man who's way too old for me

I miss sleeping with guy friends I swore I'd never kiss

Sneaking him out the back door as my roommate munches on cold pizza

Patiently awaiting the morning debrief

I miss the recklessness of youth

The euphoric bliss of a good friendship

And a group of girlfriends I thought I'd have forever

twisted broken girl

Behind all the torture,

Behind an abandoned, lonely, dark, twisted, broken girl

Sat a lost little poet, mustering up the courage to tell her story,

Years spent scribbling the same three words on dirty pages:

Let me out.

Let me out.

Let me out.

dormant crocodile

I've built a castle out of cards
Fear lives in my belly like a dormant crocodile
Waiting to snatch its next prey, I pray
To keep the pace, this race
Of a life I slayed dragons to live, I wake
In a puddle of sweat, nightmares
Forced homecomings and handcuffs
Shadows of failure dance on my walls, a reminder
Doomsday lurks around the corner

I want to return to the woods of New England
My friends will take me back with an
At least you tried, kid

fairytale fingertips

My hand slides across the couch
Your fairytale fingertips
Trace down my hips

New love
Is walking a cup of coffee
Across the room without spilling

It's also fragile, intimidating
Like we're playing a video game
With one life left
And one wrong move
Could make us start over again

But my hand melts in your palm anyway
Because this isn't a video game
And I really love coffee

daphne

Stop trying to turn them into
Something they'll never be
Move on

chaste tree

The sounds of his crash wakes me up again
Smell of pine trees and firewood fills my room
Floor-to-ceiling windows show me a Seattle skyline
The city I moved to so I could heal
I feel the weight of a hound on my legs
Warm like an oven, sleeping like a baby
Something I didn't know how badly I needed

I tiptoe my way out of my bedroom
My four-legged baby follows me
She smells like kibble and grass stains
Her snout on my thighs
Puppy snores fill my ears
I smile like a mother would
And take a deep breath that expands my belly

In this moment, I am safe
I close my eyes and remind myself
Everything is going to be okay
It has to be

....

collapse

You made my bed
Cleaned the kitchen
Held me as I was shaking
And sweating, confessing
Tales about my little life

Your blue eyes
Your *I know how hard that was*
Thanking me
For my vulnerability

I'm so sorry I squirmed
And screamed
I'm not used to being held
So lovingly

boston

Today, resentful clouds part above my messy hair—I see sun
The chains around my wrists disintegrate—I feel freedom
Warmth fills my toes, flows through my veins
A wave of forgiveness wraps my shoulders like a delicate scarf
It smells like a sea breeze, spring mornings on the south shore
It invites me under

Someone plugged me back into the wall
Now all I see is color
And all I have left to to do is
Forgive, let go
And move on

red roses

Sit by the fire with me
Take my hand
Pull me in
Take on the world with me
And whatever you do
Always come home
To me

written on a rock in new england

Jim Carrey once said

Depression is an escape

From the character you've been playing.

I can't keep up with my changes,

My phases, too many new faces.

But I'm fine on the West Coast.

Though nothing feels familiar.

A part of me

Longs to go back east.

Grow out my hair curly,

Listen to country,

Burn holes in converse.

Put more gas in this lantern,

But I'm terrified of old patterns.

I've been running from the fear of

Turning out like my father,

But I ran too far

From the girl I loved:

....

Small-town New England
Changing with the seasons,
One love she believed in.
I had so many reasons
For leaving.

What it would be like?

To smell the salt of our oceans,
See the sticky sap dripping down trees,
Feel the first fire of fall,
Hear the birds chirp
And the lawnmowers growl,
Sit at a table with friends
Who know me too well.

What would my life be like
If twelve-year-old me took the seat,
Would we have been happy?
Would I be able to sleep?
Would he have a heartbeat?
My choices still haunt me,
Yet the question—do I dare ask it?
Is it time for a homecoming?

time to go

I wish I had cinder blocks on my toes
I'm tragically bored of everyone I know
I miss the laughs from back home
And I'm starting to feel like
It's time to go

jekyll and hyde

Last night, all my therapy went out the window
Jekyll was the shell and Hyde was my soul
I transformed into the oldest version of myself
Self-righteous, indulgent, distrusting
I stormed into your sacred space when you weren't there
With a trench coat on my naked shoulders and leather gloves
A magnifying glass and a flask of Williams
I scanned the place for any trace
That you don't love me anymore

I flipped your mattress, poured out your pockets
(Two old pennies, a coffee shop receipt, gum wrappers
But you don't drink coffee—who are you buying it for?)
I white-gloved the bathroom for any sign of a mere eyelash
Scanned your dirty laundry for makeup stains or perfume

Then, I noticed you in the room, watching me
I dropped my magnifying glass, waited for the shatter
Collapsed to my knees and felt tears rush to my face
You ran to me so fast I could feel your heart race

When Hyde is in the room, you get scared too

....

advice

The most important person to trust is yourself. Trust your decisions. Trust what you want. Trust your intuition. Trust your failures. Trust your uncertainty. Trust the message life is trying to tell you. You're the only person who knows what's best for you. Turn down the voices of others trying to keep you small. Decide what you want out of life, don't let it decide for you.

safe love

You are

Stop buttons on alarm clocks

Showers after the beach

The space between summer and fall

Candles that smell like memories

And broken-in sweatshirts

You keep me safe

And let me be me

But I know

You've spent months

Trying to love me

And I don't think

I'll ever be ready

homesick

I'm writing in the corner of a Seattle café
It's been sixteen months since I moved
My friends don't visit
My family lives three thousand miles away
It's Christmas in the streets, yet it feels like Halloween
I haven't seen the sun since the summer of 2015

Conversations here consist of trauma, work, and therapy
Quiet, poetic introversion with a heaping cup of politics
Goofiness is a lost art I took for granted
Little me is proud yet disappointed
I miss walking into a room with people I know
My life is now an empty hallway: silent, safe, boring

Running away was supposed to save me
And it did for a little while
(Bittersweet impermanence)
I guess my hiding spot was never meant to be a home
Should've listened when she said
You can't put a Band-Aid on a bullet hole

cassette tapes

Dear Dad,

Before you left us, you were my favorite person. I loved being with you. You were one of the few who saw me for who I was. You understood that I was different from the rest of the kids. You knew I inherited your sadness, that I was born with your sensitivity. At three years old, I already showed signs of having a multicolored brain. That's why it's so hard to understand how you could leave me when you knew how badly I needed you. You sent into this world as a broken bird, I had no idea how to survive.

Before you got sick, I knew your love was never conditional. That's why it took decades for me to accept that this was how your story would end. That's why I did everything I could to try to get you back. You are, and forever will be, my greatest heartbreak.

There wasn't one moment when we lost you. It was a series of moments, chapters of our lives where you were going but not gone. You slowly vanished into quicksand while I broke my mind trying to pull you out. Experiencing the loss of a loved one while they're still alive feels like watching ashes fall from a cigarette—a slow burn that leads to an avoidable death.

You fought so hard for the life you built for our family, only to be the one who destroyed it. Material things and success weren't enough to outrun the monster that chased you. You were tired. You gave in. You gave up.

Why else would you take so much from me?

Unlike you, I had the courage to kill my monsters before they killed me. I can now lay down my sword and discover who I am outside the war.

I wonder what our life would look like if you were healthy. Would I call you when something broke? Would you take my car for an oil change? Would you walk me down the aisle? Would you protect me? If I sit with these questions too long—well, I never sit with these questions too long.

When I was little, I wrote you countless letters begging you to get sober. I'd leave them on your desk, car seat, and in your duffel bag. When you passed out on the couch, I'd place them on the coffee table for when you woke up. They were never acknowledged; I'm not even sure if they were read. How did you not see my pain? How could you do that to a child?

Fourteen years later, I'm writing to you while I'm three years sober. I absorbed every detail of your downfall and promised I would not let that happen to me. I would never put somebody through what you put me through.

Despite our complicated history, my favorite pieces of myself come from the best parts of you. I know how to make a table of friends throw their heads back in laughter. I'm passionate about music and pay attention to the lyrics like you do. My heart is too big for my mind, like yours. I fearlessly pave my own way, like you tried to.

This generational pain we've both carried is going to end with me. These pieces of our lives will take their highest form—art.

I want you to know it's okay to let go. I have found forgiveness in the wreckage, and I forgive you.

Please watch over me when you go.

I love you.

M

poetry

My world turned into a Sunday afternoon

With nothing to do but everything

I turned down the noise

Heard my voice

And fell in love with the words

margaret michelle

I know we haven't formally met
And you're probably wondering
Why it took me so long
To journey back here
And save you

I know we look alike, so I'll explain
Motherhood was a task too large for a child
It was my mission to gather everything I needed
To find you and be who you needed

I kneel with the kindest smile
And pull a jeweled locket from my pocket
Colorful fairies dance around the golden rim
Her eyes light up with wonder
And she starts to understand this is hers
This is ours
For me? You mean it?

I tell her
This will be your new destiny, and I promise

LET ME OUT

If you're hungry, I will feed you
If you're scared, I will listen to you
If you're angry, I will ask, learn, and understand
If you're crying, I will let you
If you want to go home, I won't make you to stay
If you're insecure, I will build you up
If you're lost, I will come find you
I will always come find you

She opens her tiny arms
And I hug her into my chest
A maternal surge through my heart

I promise to be everything we needed
When we were this young

afterlife

We met a lifetime ago
At a 1920s speakeasy
You with your snakeskin fedora
Me in black fishnet stockings
And kitten heels
You ordered me a whiskey
I sipped shyly
Listening to your crazy stories
We both smoked long cigarettes
Smoke curled up to the ceiling
And I knew I wasn't leaving

We met at a café in the 1950s
You came in every day
Noticed me sitting by myself reading
It took you a couple of weeks
To muster up the courage to buy me coffee
But when you did
We sat at that café till closing

We met at Woodstock in 1969
My blonde hair traveled down my back
Yours sat shoulder length, you were shirtless
Sweaty, dirty, two free spirited hippies
Swaying to the music
In our own universe
Not together but never apart

And in 2025, we meet at a book signing
Fall is in the air, I'm approaching thirty
Somehow, someway we're both from Boston
Two adults answering life's questions
And when I look into those curious eyes
There is not a stranger in front of me
It's a familiarity that needs no explanation
You are the next person
That will be written on these pages

marigold

Life took the one person I truly loved

Who I never allowed myself to love

letters never sent XIII

MARCH 2023

Dear B,

It's been 365 days since you left us. I've flown home more times in the last year than I have in the last 10. My mindset shifted from 'anywhere but home' to 'nowhere is better than home.' Admittedly, I hate living in a city. You would be mortified at this high-rise I am perched in right now, suffocating me as I write.

I've spent the last few months turning over rocks and looking for answers, begging for reasons as to why you had to leave. My heart breaks a little more every time I hear how much pain you were in. When I'm home, I'll go sit by the water at our favorite spot, bring flowers to your grave, and drive around our town working through the noise in my head. One visit, I left you a poem underneath a rock; I still wonder if anyone found it.

Grieving you is like sailing in the middle of a storm, not knowing if I'll ever reach land again. I sit with mediums to talk to you directly, read books about signs from the spirits, and have spent

....

many lonely city nights crying into this unfamiliar skyline. Before I fall asleep, I recount my day to you in my mind. I swear I can hear you talking back. Since you're passing, I haven't had a day where I do not think about you.

You're in the sleepy sunsets, the old farm trucks, and starry night smoke sessions. You're with me constantly, and I look for you in everyone. I feel you pulling me back home, whether that means back to Boston or back to myself, I'm unsure. I have strayed so far from who I used to be. But I can't help but notice country music playing in my car again, a sudden desire to be barefoot in a field, and a craving to make people laugh. This season, I'm looking forward to finding the perfect sundress and purchasing a fresh pair of red converse.

I've learned so much in these last twelve months. Most of my life, I didn't know how to love anything, including you. Especially you. I never let myself feel how painful it was for me to let us go. I never acknowledged how painful it was for you to continuously watch me, feel me, let me disappear.

One thing I do know now is that we were never crazy for feeling this way about each other; we were just too young to handle it. Up against our own stubbornness, family politics, addictions – what child is equipped? Youth is a disease from which only one of us managed to recover.

If you were here, you would tell me, 'Come home so we can get married.' And after years of asking me this question, I would happily say yes.

<u>*Perhaps there are endless reasons why we never figured it out.* </u> *If we ended up together, it probably would've been madness, chaotic, and irresponsible. We would've fought like crazy. We would've crashed and burned, ending up hating each other. Our families would've never accepted our relationship. You'd be pulling me back, and I'd be pulling you forward. We'd spend decades wrapped up in a toxic love that never felt safe. If we got together that summer night, it would've been two unhealed souls trying to love each other – a recipe for a heartbreak we couldn't recover from.*

Or maybe it would've been worse than all of that: we would've been deliriously happy. I would've flown you to Seattle to help me pack up and move back home. You'd be making me a cup of coffee right now, and I would be writing you a morning love poem. The fire would be crackling, and country music would be playing. Life would feel colorful again, and I'd have a tiny little ring on my finger. Our families would've loved each other, and the holidays would be full and hilarious. We'd spend summers on the boat and winters in Vermont. We would get married at the courthouse because we couldn't wait a second longer for our forever.

Losing you is desperation. I am desperate for a different ending to this story.

We were the same people, B. We always have been. Emotionally driven, romantic creatures, living in a world of black and white film. You only get a few people in this life who understand you without explanation. You were one of mine. Thank you for never making me feel like I had to be anyone else. For loving me in the rare moments I was myself. You are one of the happiest parts of my youth.

I'm so sorry I wasn't there to help you. I wasn't there to let you out.

I'm so sorry I never wrote these letters when it mattered.

I'm sure you don't remember this, but a few weeks before I went to college, we were on our way to a Red Sox game on a hot summer day. You rolled down the window, stuck your hand out, tilted your head back, and said, 'Meg, the trees. Look at the trees. I love the trees. Don't you love them?'

You were one of the greatest loves of my life, my twin flame, the person I meet in every lifetime.

I know wherever you are, it is summer all the time.

I miss you.

I love you.

I will never stop writing to you.

See you in the next life, B.

Meg

morning love poem

You love me in light
Walk with me in blue
I own your midnights
Baby, you're brand new

Now
Your chest is where I sleep
Doe eyes, freckled cheeks
I have everything I need
When you're next to me

3:43 AM

It's better to think you're right and be proved wrong than to tell yourself something is wrong and learn that you were right.

There were so many things I had right. Why did I think everyone knew better than me?

lily of the valley

I love the way my hair falls down my back
A gift from my parents
I love my self-awareness
Like a warrior surveying the land
I'm radically honest with my reflection
Love the way my face is filled out and warm
I could run my hands through the river of blood
That flows through me
Full of life and curiosity

I love my creativity
I'm an artist of possibility

I love that my biggest fear is hurting feelings
I've slept with pain but work hard not to cause it

I love the way I know what I'm doing even when I don't
If I fail, I fail forward, learning the lesson designed for me
I love my comfort with the uncomfortable
I see chaos as an opportunity
Heartache as a growing pain

....

Pain as a promise of a better life

I love the way I listen to what life tells me

I'm unafraid to take risks

Like a cliff diver off the coasts of Australia, I will jump eventually

I'm the detective in my own life

Turning over every rock until I stand confident in my divinity

I love the way I'm not afraid to start new projects

See new cities or meet new people

Newness is a friend I welcome into my home

I love the way I write with vengeance and vulnerability

If I ever make history, I hope my story will be

She lived her life in poetry

another saturday morning

Arm covering cold sheets

Blinking eyes open

No one

This bed feels like an ocean

I'm the only one floating

For miles

I've been walking alone

People slipping through fingers

Disappearing

Like snowflakes on pavement

Filled with heartbreak yet

Shrugged at the goodbye

Loneliness is a constant

But this readiness?

Cleared spaces in my soul

....

LET ME OUT

Waiting to love someone

Is an unfamiliar language

I don't know how to speak

sweetpea

With each passing year, I heard it
I heard it in the dusty bars of Charleston
Past the revolving door of men I couldn't cling to
In the liquor that never got me drunk enough
To drown it out, tune it out

I felt it in the streets of our hometown
Sitting on my mother's rooftop
Hoping to see your truck pass by
I knew it in 2011, 2015, 2017, 2019, and 2022
I saw it in the loneliness of North Carolina
The empty highways in the Midwest
The sunsets in Arizona
The storms of Seattle
I knew it at the height of my sobriety
In the palms of my hands

And then it screamed so loud
I covered my ears and screamed back
Excruciating wails

....

LET ME OUT

Pierced my ghost-like apartment
Sent me into the fetal position
I believed it would kill me
And it did
It still does
Just one sentence, one feeling, repeatedly:
You were one of the greatest loves of my life

hydrangeas

Being my father's daughter
Made my mother a stranger

3:59 AM

Find a life you don't need escaping from. Find people who allow you to self-express and be yourself. Find a love that is gentle, consistent, and filled to the brim with adventure. Find family outside the one that was given to you.

Find reasons to stay. Look for it in your morning coffee, fresh flowers, the love of an animal, and the way grass feels on your bare feet.

I promise, the pain wasn't for nothing. You are not responsible for what happened to you, but you are responsible for healing from it.

The life you want is out there, waiting. What you are looking for, will look for you too.

We want you here. I want you here.

You are a piece of us, and we will be incomplete without you.

We all deserve to be loved at full capacity.

encore

I am standing barefoot in this empty apartment.

There are no words left in me. This journey is complete.

If you've made it this far, thank you.

It is not the end; it is only the beginning.

It's finally time to *let me out*.

And I can only hope,

I'll be able to *let me be*.

Acknowledgements

These writings were my lifeline during a time when I felt like I was withering away. The pieces kept me grounded in sobriety and helped me decipher the intricacies of my mind. To those who stood by me during this process, I am eternally grateful. Even when I was at my most challenging, your unwavering support kept me afloat.

Emily – my meticulous and encouraging editor, you were the first person I allowed to read my work, and you welcomed me with open arms. Thank you for taking care of this project as if it were your own and for coaching me every step of the way.

Vanessa, Lucy – my best friends. I am convinced we were together long before this life started. Thank you for being delusionally supportive. You are friendship through all stages of life. Thank you for making me laugh until my cheeks hurt, for turning insane ideas into timeless stories, and for our endless adventures. You are my soulmates, my greatest cheerleaders. I love you so much.

AJ - This life hasn't swallowed me whole because of you. Thank you for defending me in times when I can't defend myself. Thank you for pushing me to reach my greatest potential, even at times when I resist. Thank you for your home-cooked meals, your warm blankets, and your willingness to listen to me endlessly. Thank you for bringing me out to Seattle. Without this place, I don't think I could've finished this book or healed as quickly. I love you.

Mom & Dad – I can only hope you see the beauty in this.

And to all the characters, both big and small, thank you for being a part of this story.

Till next time,

MJ

About The Author

MJ is an inspiring writer from a small town south of Boston. Her journey has been marked by triumph over adversity, as she battled substance abuse for years before finding solace in sobriety just two weeks into the pandemic. It was during the early days of her healing process, when emotions were overwhelming, that MJ turned to writing as a form of catharsis.

Her debut collection, LET ME OUT, emerged because of this emotional release. Through her personal narratives, MJ aims to reach young adults who have slipped through the cracks in our broken systems. She delves into topics such as substance abuse in young children, generational traumas, and the quest for self-expression in a world that often seeks to make people invisible.

Presently, she lives in Seattle, surrounded by flowers with her hound-dog, Theo. Johnson devotes most of her time to writing, stages, and social media, where she connects with audiences through her unique brand of storytelling and humor. Through comedy, she continues to share more daily aspects of her life, weaving together tales that resonate with those who have walked similar paths.

MJ Johnson's work is a testament to the power of personal growth, resilience, and the ability to find light even in the darkest of times.

@ mjswaycreative

....